AHIMAN

A REVIEW OF MASONIC CULTURE & TRADITION

EDITED BY

SHAWN EYER

I

6009

Plumbstone | 2009

AHIMAN

A Review of Masonic Culture & Tradition

*Devoted to excellence
in Masonic education,
research, philosophy
arts and literature.*

Shawn Eyer

EDITOR

Erik Arneson
Chris Ellis
Jeremy Gross

PROOFREADING

Plumbstone
SAN FRANCISCO

http://www.plumbstone.com

ISBN 978-1-60302-365-8

Contents

Introduction   1

FEATURES   A Spiritual Vision of   30
the Liberal Arts and Sciences
Thomas D. Worrel

The Memory Lodge: 62
Practicing the Art of Memory
Erik L. Arneson

The Allegory of the Cave   72
Plato

Thomas Starr King: Apostle   89
of Liberty, Brother of the Craft
Adam G. Kendall

Silence and Solemnity   102
in Craft Freemasonry
Shawn Eyer

LODGE PAPERS   An Angle of Perfect Sincerity   12
Shawn Eyer

Masonic Initiation & Plato's   79
Allegory of the Cave
David E. Stafford

LITERATURE   Jabbok   121
Erik O'Neal

VERSE

Before Dawn   11
Shawn Eyer

Charge   29
Greg Maier

A Lodge Salutatory   71
Robert G. Davis

A Song of Degrees: The Aspirant   88
W. L. Wilmshurst

First Initiation   120
Mounir Hanafi

CLASSIC ARTICLES   The Vision of Ahiman   5
Lawrence Dermott, 1756

The Geometry of Character   20
Joseph Fort Newton, 1927

Our Conscious Temple   94
Thomas Starr King, 1863

REVIEWS   JULIAN REES   126
Tracing Boards of the Three Degrees
in Craft Freemasonry Explained
Shawn Eyer

HENRIK BOGDAN   132
Western Esotericism and Rituals of Initiation
Brian Hodges

About the Contributors   135
Image Credits   136
Index   137

Introduction

Shawn Eyer

It is with tremendous pleasure that I introduce the first volume of Plumbstone's *Ahiman* — an anthology dedicated to Masonic ritual, symbolism, philosophy, art and research. Our development of the new journal began several years ago, when we realized the need for a philosophically-based review of Masonic studies.

Although much of the rhetoric within Freemasonry during the past several decades has focused upon ways in which the Masonic ritual and overall Lodge experience might be streamlined or minimized in an attempt to appeal to the perceived desires of a modern audience, it soon became evident that the defining characteristic of twenty-first century Freemasons was that they tend to desire *more, not less*, from the Craft. If anything, today's candidate for our fraternity has grown increasingly interested in a deeper experience of Masonic symbolism. Now, brethren seek a Craft that is more relevant in their lives, and more challenging to their hearts and minds.

A growing number of Lodges are working to address these needs through improved educational programs and a more deliberate approach to candidate instruction. Several Grand Lodges have issued new Masonic education guidelines, often greatly improved over what had previously been available.

Ahiman: A Review of Masonic Culture & Tradition is designed to support these positive efforts by providing a venue for thoughtful articles on Craft symbolism, history, and meaning. It is our goal to foster a well-rounded approach to Masonic education, where the traditions of the past

are respectfully honored, and the speculations of the present are responsible, well-researched and thought-provoking. By establishing an accessible medium for high-quality, medium-length articles that are interpretive (rather than strictly historical) in nature, *Ahiman* is intended to serve a need that has been long unmet in the literature of speculative Freemasonry.

Ahiman in Ancient & Masonic Legend

Some explanation of the journal's name may be in order. The publication is named AHIMAN in honor of a legendary character in Masonic literature. In ancient times, the name Ahiman would be written 𐤀𐤄𐤉𐤌𐤍 (*aḥimn*) and pronounced "ah–*khee*–mahn." The word literally means "right-hand brother." In the Volume of the Sacred Law, there are two characters named Ahiman: the first, an Anakite occupying Hebron, who is conquered by Caleb (Numbers 13:22, Joshua 15:14); later tradition specifies that he was a giant (e.g., Josephus, *Antiquities* 3.14; Babylonian Talmud, *Yoma* 10a, *Sotah* 34b). But the Ahiman who is relevant Masonically is a later figure—one of a group of Levites appointed by King David to serve a special function in the Jerusalem sanctuary:

> The gatekeepers were Shallum, Akkub, Talmon, Ahiman; and their kindred Shallum was the chief…. These were the gatekeepers of the camp of the Levites.
>
> Shallum son of Kore… and his kindred of his

ancestral house, the Korahites, were in charge of the work of the service, guardians of the thresholds of the tent, as their ancestors had been in charge of the camp of the LORD, guardians of the entrance.

All these, who were chosen as gatekeepers at the thresholds, were two hundred twelve. They were enrolled by genealogies in their villages. David and the seer Samuel established them in their office of trust. So they and their descendants were in charge of the gates of the house of the LORD, that is, the house of the tent, as guards.

The gatekeepers were on the four sides, east, west, north, and south…. [T]he four chief gatekeepers, who were Levites, were *in charge of the chambers and the treasures of the house of God.* And they would spend the night near the house of God; for on them lay the duty of watching, and they had charge of opening it every morning.

Some of them had charge of the utensils of service…. Others of them were appointed over the furniture, and over all the holy utensils, also over the choice flour [i.e., the corn], the wine, the oil, the incense, and the spices. Others, of the sons of the priests, prepared the mixing of the spices, and [another] was in charge of making the flat cakes. (1 Chronicles 9: 17–19, 22–31 NRSV)

It is easy to see why the *shomrei ha-saf* or "guardians of the threshold" were of interest to early Freemasons. They had charge of the corn, wine and oil offerings at the Temple, and were *recipients* of some of them. They also kept the ritual space of the Temple guarded. This connects, in speculative Freemasonry, to the emblematic wages of a Mason, and the "most important duty" of tiling the Lodge. The importance of having a trustworthy brother to guard the four main gates of the Temple is obvious to every Master Mason.

LAURENCE DERMOTT'S STORY OF AHIMAN

These traditions were likely the inspiration for the Antients' fascination with the guardians, manifested most obviously in the title which the Antient Grand Lodge of England used for their book of constitutions: *Ahiman Rezon, or A Help to a Brother.* It first appeared in 1756, and many jurisdictions still call their printed constitutions by that name.

In *Ahiman Rezon*, Lawrence Dermott—the Antients' indefatigable Grand Secretary—records the deliberably amusing story (reprinted verbatim in this volume, pp. 5–10) of his attempt to write a history of Freemasonry. This would be the Antients' version of the history that James Anderson had composed for the Moderns' constitutions in 1723. Dermott facetiously boasted: "I began to flourish away in a most admirable Manner…. I imagined myself superior to Josephus, Stackhouse, or any other Historian…."

But just as Dermott was finishing, he wrote that he "insensibly fell into a Slumber," whereon it seemed that four men, dressed and speaking in an ancient way, appeared in his room. He asked them their names, and they answered:

"We are four Brothers, and come from the holy City of Jerusalem; our Names are Shallum, Ahiman, Akhub, and Talmon. […] The wise king Solomon, Grand Master of Israel, appointed us head Porters at the Temple…and therefore we can give a full and particular Description of that wonderful Fabrick, and likewise of the ingenious Artists who perform'd it."

A footnote in the original identifies the four as the same characters mentioned in the passage from 1 Chronicles cited earlier. When Dermott asks their assistance with his history book, Ahiman scoffs that while many have attempted to write parts thereof, even including the spiritual meanings of the tradition, none of the results have been comprehensive. But he tells Dermott that he knows "an eminent Brother who can inform you in every Particular that is necessary to your present Undertaking." At that, the High Priest from the Temple appears, clad in a breastplate so radiant that Dermott is blinded until it is covered up.

The High Priest examines Dermott's history and finds it quite inadequate. The High Priest affirms that while the Masons who built Solomon's Temple were the most skilled kabbalists (students of the Jewish esoteric tradition) of their time, Masonic histories tended to ignore them—the real bearers of "the whole Mystery"—in order to concentrate upon powerful men bearing lofty titles, whose only contribution was giving orders for various projects.

Ahiman and the High Priest convince Dermott to take another approach, discarding his history. The importance of this "vision" is generally overlooked. Here, the Antients rejected the Moderns' attempt to place their version of Freemasonry at the center of human history, with not only Moses and Solomon, but Nebuchadnezar, Augustus Caesar and many other kings and rulers as "Grand Masters." Instead, Dermott's account proposed that the real work of Masonry was kabbalistic in nature and practiced through the years by mostly *unknown* individuals, numbering in the thousands, whom he calls "the faithful Crafts."

The subtitle of the 1756 *Ahiman Rezon* was "A Help to a Brother," and, in light of the story related above, probably ought to be understood as referring to the aid that Ahiman rendered to Dermott in helping him to change his Masonic priorities, away from what was seen as the Moderns' fixation upon worldly fame, to the more essential and spiritual lessons of the "whole Mystery" of the Craft.

Integrating Masonic Scholarship & Philosophy

The Antients' legend of Ahiman is a powerful and relevant story for today's Freemasons who are desirous of shifting their own priorities to examine not merely the history of Freemasonry, but its meaning as well. It shows us that some of the same debates that concern today's fraternity were there even in the eighteenth century, well before our rituals had finished developing into their classical form.

Thus, the name of *Ahiman: A Review of Masonic Culture & Tradition* is intended to reflect our interest in integrating the neglected studies of philosophy and symbolism with a scholarly approach. This is a new kind of Masonic publication, seeking to transcend the rigid definitions and false dichotomies that have for too long constrained what is written about Masonic history, ritual, symbolism, art and literature, and ultimately to create new venues for the exploration and promotion of Masonic culture.

Through established media such as *Ars Quatuor Coronatorum* and *Heredom*, historians of Freemasonry have long enjoyed the benefits of an ongoing, progressive scholarly conversation. One writer's work builds upon another's, and over time the common understanding of the subject advances.

But the same has not exactly been true for the speculative side of Freemasonry. One of the purposes of *Ahiman* is to promulgate a scholarly approach among those who explore Masonic philosophy, and to encourage such writers to engage in a long-term conversation with their peers, as well as with the established disciplines of academic historical research. By distinguishing between mythic language and historiography, this conversation will be greatly enhanced.

Structure & Format

The format of *Ahiman* is designed to support the overall mission of the anthology to encourage the integration of Masonic philosophy, research, tradition and practice. *Ahiman* is the only English-language publication that is exclusively devoted to art, literature, and scholarly articles that reflect this focus.

RESEARCH ARTICLES

A primary feature of each volume of *Ahiman* will be research articles that focus on Masonic ritual, symbolism and philosophy. With a flexible page count, the anthology can accommodate meritorious articles of any length.

VISUAL ARTS & LITERATURE

Literary endeavors relating to Freemasonry have lacked a natural medium for some time. *Ahiman's* format includes poetry and short fiction that is of high quality and that reinforces the mission of the journal. And, *Ahiman* is printed in color so that the artistic impact of drawings, paintings and photography may be best communicated.

LODGE TALKS

In each volume, *Ahiman* will present some articles of suitable length and style to be read in lodge education programs. In the classical phase of the development of speculative Freemasonry, many lodges were places of learning, where lectures took place on Freemasonry and other subjects. Today, some wish to revive that tradition. *Ahiman* directly addresses this issue by providing stimulating presentations, and by encouraging more authors to produce them.

CLASSIC ARTICLES

As we engage in Masonic discourse and celebrate the culture of Freemasonry, we strengthen what our ancient brethren liked to call the Mystic Tie. This was understood as more than merely the favorable sentiment one naturally feels in the company of worthy brethren — it is the cultural, experiential and spiritual connection that all regular Masons feel toward one another, completely independent of the constraints of location and time. In the spirit of forging a stronger Masonic culture and a more vivid perception of the Mystic Tie, *Ahiman* will feature relevant and interesting examples of writing from each century of the Craft's rich literary history.

REVIEWS

Ahiman offers high quality, reliable reviews of books (and works in other media) written by careful, qualified reviewers. Our reviews will be in-depth and critical while presented in an accessible style.

Ahiman is published according to the material received, with no formal interval between volumes. At this time, it is expected that no more than one volume will appear during a given calendar year.

The anthology welcomes high-quality submissions in all of the above categories. Honorariums are offered to the contributors of accepted features. To make a proposal, simply use the appropriate contact feature on the Plumbstone website. ⨍

The Vision of Ahiman

Lawrence Dermott

In light of the name adopted for this journal, it seems fitting to reproduce the Masonic literary origin of Ahiman. In this humorous yet also very serious account, Laurence Dermott — the original Grand Secretary of the Antient Grand Lodge of England — explains why his masterwork does not, in contrast with other similar works such as Anderson's *Constitutions* of 1723, contain a grandiose history of the Craft tracing it from Adam to the current Grand Master. This withering satire against what he saw as the pretensions of the "Moderns" may even be the original "dog ate my homework" story. However, it is also a carefully written account which hints at the true, more mystical side of the Craft as Dermott saw it. — Ed.

I T HAS BEEN the general Custom of all my worthy Brethren, who have honoured the Craft with their Books of Constitutions, or Pocket-Companions for Free-Masons, to give us a long and pleasing History of Masonry from the Creation to the Time of their writing and publishing such Accounts, *viz.* from *Adam* to *Noah*, from *Noah* to *Nimrod*, from *Nimrod* to *Solomon*, from *Solomon* to *Cyrus*, from *Cyrus* to *Seleucus Nicator*, from *Seleucus Nicator*, to *Augustus Cæsar*, from *Augustus Cæsar* to the Havock of the Goths, and so on until the Revival of the *Augustan* Style, *&c. &c. &c.* Wherein they give us an Account of the drawing, scheming, planning, designing, erecting, and building of Temples, Towers, Cities, Castles, Palaces, Theatres, Pyramids, Monuments, Bridges, Walls, Pillars, Courts, Halls, Fortifications, and Labyrinths, with the famous Light-house of *Pharos* and Colossus of *Rhodes*, and many other wonderful works performed by the ARCHITECTS, to the great Satisfaction of the Readers, and Edification of Free-Masons.[1]

Having called to Mind the old Proverb, *Better be out of the World than out of Fashion*, I was fully determined to write an History of Masonry, whereby I did expect to give the World an uncommon Satisfaction; in order to enable myself to execute this great Design, I purchased all or most of the Histories, Constitutions, Pocket-Companions, and other Pieces (on that Subject) now extant in the *English* Tongue.

My next step was to furnish myself with a sufficient quantity of pens, ink and paper: this being done, I immediately fancied myself an HISTORIAN, and intended to trace Masonry not only to *Adam*, in his sylvan Lodge in *Paradise*, but to give some account of the Craft even before the Creation: and (as a Foundation) I placed the following Works round about me, so as to be convenient to have Recourse to them as Occasion should require, *viz.* Dr. *Anderson* and Mr. *Spratt*, before me, Dr. *D'Assigny* and Mr. *Smith*, on my Right-hand, Dr. *Desagulier* and Mr. *Pennell* on my Left-hand, and Mr. *Scott* and Mr. *Lyon* behind me: a Copy of (that often called) the Original Constitutions (said to be in the Possession of Mr. *John Clark*, in *Paris*), and another Copy of the same Magnitude handed about in *England*, together with the Pamphlets printed at *Frankfort* in *Germany*, I tied up in the Public Advertiser of *Friday, October 19, 1753*, and threw them under the table.

Having tried my Pen, and wrote a Line not unlike the Beginning of the Chapter in the Alcoran[2], I began to flourish away in a most admirable Manner, and in a few Days wrote the first Volume of the History of Masonry, wherein was a full account of the Transactions of the first Grand Lodge, particularly the excluding of the unruly Members, as related by Mr. *Milton*.[3]

By this Time I imagined myself superior to *Josephus*, *Stackhouse*, or any other Historian whom the Reader shall please to think on. And as I intended to give the World a History of Masonry for several Years before the Creation, I made no Manner of doubt but my Work should live at least two thousand Years after the general Conflagration. Perhaps some of my Readers (I mean those that are best acquainted with my Capacity) will say, he has more Vanity than Wit; and as to Learning, it is as great a Stranger to him, as Free-Masonry is to Women; yet he has the folly to think himself an Historian, and expects to become a great Man, *&c.* Whether such an Opinion be true or false, it matters nought to me; for the World must allow, that (tho' no

Man has found out the perpetual Motion) all Men ever had, have now, and ever will have a perpetual Notion: And furthermore, we read, that the following Persons, so much famed in History, were not only poor Men, but many of them of a very mean extraction. The wise Philosopher *Socrates*, was the Son of a poor Stone-carver; the tragic Poet *Euripides*, was the son of poor Parents; as was *Demosthenes*, the honour of Greek eloquence; *Virgil*, the famous Latin Poet, was the Son of a poor Mantuan labouring Potter; *Horace*, the incomparable Lyric, was the Son of a Trumpeter in the wars; *Tarquinius Priscus*, King of the *Romans*, was the Son of a Merchant; and *Servius Tullius*, another King of the Romans, was begotten on a Woman Slave; *Septimius Severus*, is said to come of a very base Degree; *Agathocles*, King of Sicily, was a Potter's Son; *Elius Pertinax* was a poor Artificer, or, as some say, a simple Seller of Wood; the Parents of *Venadius Bassus*, are said to be very miserable poor People; and *Arsaces*, King of the Parthians, was of so mean and obscure Parentage, that no Man's memory could make a report of his Father or Mother; *Ptolomy* King of Egypt, was the son of a Squire in *Alexander's* Army; the Emperor *Dioclesian*, was the Son of a Scrivener; the Emperor *Probus* was Son of a Gardener; and the Parents of *Aurelius*, were so obscure that Writers have not agreed who they were; *Maximus* was the Son of a Smith, or as some say a Waggon-Wright; *Marcus Julius Licinius*, was the Son of a Herdsman; *Bonosus* was the Son of a poor stipendary Schoolmaster; *Mauritus Justinus*, predecessor to *Justinian*, and also *Galerus*, were both Shepherds; Pope *John*, the twenty-second of that Name, was the Son of a Shoe-Maker; Pope *Nicholas* the fifth was the Son of a Man that sold Eggs and Butter about the Streets; and Pope *Sixtus* the Fourth was a Mariner's Son; *Lamusius*, King of the Lombards, was the Son of a common Strumpet, who (when he was an Infant) threw him into a Ditch, but was taken out by King *Agelmond*; *Primislaus,* king of *Bohemia*, was the son of a country Peasant; *Tamerlane* the Great was a Herdsman; *Caius Marius,* seven times Consul of *Rome*, was born of poor Parents in the Village of *Apirnum*; and *Marcus Tullius Cicero*, Consul of *Rome*, and Pro-Consul in *Asia*, was from the poor *Tugriole* of *Arpinum*, the meanest Parentage that could be; *Ventidius,* Field-Marshal and Consul of *Rome*, was the Son of a Muleteer; and *Thophrastus* was the son of a Botcher, *i.e.* a Mender of Garments, *&c.*

I have heard of many Others of later Date (not so far distant as *Fequin*[4]) that have been preferred to Places or Offices of great Trust, and dignified with Titles of Honour, without having the least Claim to Wit, Courage, Learning or Honesty; therefore, if such Occurrences be duly considered, I humbly conceive it will not be deemed as a capital Offence, that I should entertain my own perpetual Notion, while I do not endeavor to disinherit any Man of his Properties.

I doubt I have tired the Reader's Patience; and if so, I humbly beg his Pardon for this long

Digression. But to return: While my Mind was wholly taken up with my fancied Superiority as an Historian, &c. I insensibly fell into a Slumber, when me-thought four Men entered my Room; their Habits appeared to be of very ancient Fashion, and their Language also I imagined to be either *Hebrew*, *Arabic*, or *Chaldean*, in which they addressed me, and I immediately answered them after the Pantomime Fashion: After some formal Ceremonies, I desired to know their Names, and from whence they came; to which one of them answered me (in *English*) We are four Brothers, and come from the holy City of *Jerusalem*; our Names are *Shallum*, *Ahiman*, *Akhub*, and *Talmon*. Hearing they were sojourners from Jerusalem, I asked them whether they could give any account of SOLOMON'S TEMPLE; to which *Shallum*[5] (the chief of them) made Answer and said, The wise KING SOLOMON, GRAND MASTER of *Israel*, appointed us head Porters at the Temple, in the thirty-second Year of his Age, the twelfth of his Reign, and about the Year of the World 2942; and therefore we can give a full and particular Description of that wonderful Fabrick, and likewise of the ingenious Artists who perform'd it.

I was glad to meet with such Brethren, from whom I did expect a great deal of Knowledge; which the many Ages they had lived in must have taught them, if their Memories did not fail: Upon this Consideration I told them, that I was writing a History of Masonry, and beg'd their Assistance, &c.

A History of Masonry! (says *Ahiman*) from the Day of the Dedication of the Holy Temple to this present Time, I have not seen a History of Masonry, though some have pretended (not only) to describe the Length, Breadth, Height, Weight, Colour, Shape, Form, and Substance of every Thing within and about the Temple; but also to tell the spiritual[6] Meaning of them, as

if they knew the Mind of him who gave Orders for that Building, or seen it finished: but I can assure you that such Surveyors have never seen the Temple, nay never have been within a thousand Miles of *Jerusalem*[7]: Indeed (continued he) there was one *Flavius* (I think he was a soldier)[8] took a great deal of Notice of the Temple, and other Matters about it; as did another Man named *Jerry*: There were two others, whose Names I have forgot, but remember one of them was an excellent Dreamer,[9] and the other was very handy in collecting all Manner of good Writings[10] after the Captivity.

Those were the only Men that have wrote most and best upon that Subject, and yet all their Works together would not be sufficient for a Preface to the History of Masonry; but for your further Instructions, you shall hear an eminent Brother who can inform you in every Particular that is necessary to your present Undertaking. The Words were scarce ended, when there appeared a grave old Gentleman, with a long Beard; he was dressed in an embroidered Vest, and wore a Breast-Plate of Gold, set with twelve precious Stones, which formed an oblong Square: I was informed that the Name of the Stones were *Sardine, Emerald, Ligure, Beryl, Topas, Saphire, Agate, Onyx, Carbuncle, Diamond, Amethyst*, and *Jasper*: Upon these Stones were engraved the Names of the twelve Tribes, viz. *Reuben, Judah, Gad, Zebulun, Simeon, Dan, Asher, Joseph, Levi, Naphthali, Issacher*, and *Benjamin*.[11]

Upon his Entrance, the four Sojourners did him the Homage due to a Superior; as to me, the Lustre of his Breast-Plate dazzled my Sight, in such a Manner that I could scarce look at him. But *Ahiman* giving him to understand that the People of this Country were weak-sighted, he immediately covered his Breast-Plate; which not only gave me an Opportunity of perceiving him more distinct, but also of paying him my Respects in the best Manner I was capable of; and making a very low Bow, I presented him with the first Volume of the History of Masonry, hoped he would do me the Honor of perusing it, and beg'd his Advice for my further Proceedings: He kindly received it, and read it over, whilst I impatiently waited to hear his Opinion; which at last (to my Mortification) amounted to no more than an old *Hebrew* Proverb (which *Ahiman* translated thus: *Thou hast div'd deep into the Water, and hast brought up a Potsherd*): Nevertheless he took me by the Hand, and said [12]; My Son, if thou wilt thou shalt be taught, and if thou wilt apply thy Mind thou shalt be witty; if thou love to hear, thou shalt receive (Doctrine); and if thou delight in hearing thou shalt be wise: And although your History of Masonry is not worth Notice, yet you may write many other Things of great Service to the Fraternity.

Certain it is (continued he) that Free-Masonry has been from the Creation (though not under that Name); that it was a divine Gift from GOD; that *Cain* and the Builders of his City were Strangers to the secret Mystery of Masonry; that there were but four Masons in the World when the Deluge happened; that one of the four, even the second Son of *Noah*, was not Master of the art; that *Nimrod*, nor any of his Bricklayers, knew any thing of the Matter; and that there were but very few Masters of the Art (even) at *Solomon's* Temple: Whereby it plainly appears, that the whole Mystery was communicated to very few at that Time; that at *Solomon's* Temple (and not before) it received the name of Free-Masonry, because the Masons at *Jerusalem* and *Tyre* were the greatest Cabalists [13] then in the World; that the Mystery has been, for the most part practised amongst Builders since *Solomon's* Time; that there were some hundreds mentioned (in Histories of Masonry) under the Titles of Grand-Masters, &c. for no other Reason than that of giving Orders for the Building of a House, Tower, Castle, or some other Edifice (or perhaps for suffering the Masons to erect such in their territories, &c.) while the Memories of as many Thousands of the faithful Crafts are buried in Oblivion: From whence he gave me

> IF THOU WILT thou shalt be taught, and if thou wilt apply thy mind thou shalt be witty; if thou love to hear, thou shalt receive; and if thou delight in hearing thou shalt be wise.
>
> —Ben Sirach

to understand, that such Histories were of no Use to the Society at present; and further added, that the Manner of constituting Lodges, the old and new Regulations, &c. were the only and most useful Things (concerning Free-Masonry) that could be wrote: To which I beg'd to be informed, whether Songs were to be introduced: His Answer was [14]: *If thou be made the Master, lift not thyself up; but be among them as one of the rest: Take diligent Care for them, and so sit down.*

And when thou hast done all thy Duty, sit down, that thou mayst be merry with them; and receive a Crown for thy good Behaviour.

Speak thou that art the elder, for it becometh thee; but with sound Judgment: and hinder not Music.

And at all Times let thy Garments be White. [15]

While he was speaking these last Words, I was awakened by a young Puppy that (got into the room while I slept, and, seizing my Papers, eat a great part of them, and) was then (between my Legs) shaking and tearing the last Sheet of what I had wrote.

I have not Words to express the Sorrow, Grief, Trouble and Vexation I was in, upon seeing the Catastrophe of a Work which I expected would outlast the Teeth of Time.

Like one distracted (as in Truth I was) I ran to the Owner of the Dog, and demanded immediate Satisfaction: He told me he would hang the Cur; but at the same Time he imagined I should be under more Obligation to him for so doing, than he was to me for what had happened.

In short, I looked upon it as a bad Omen; and my late dream had made so great an Impression on my Mind, that Superstition got the better of me and caused me to deviate from the general Custom of my worthy predecessors; otherwise I would have published a History of Masonry: and as this is rather an accidental than a designed Fault, I hope the Reader will look over it with a favourable Eye. ⨍

לאר נצ רר מיה סופר

Lau: Dermott

Notes

Grand Secretary Dermott's signature is reproduced from the minute book of the Grand Lodge of the Antients, 1757. After his name written phonetically in Hebrew characters, Dermott has included a Hebrew title, *sofer*, which means "scribe." It is reasonable to believe that he intended this as the Hebrew version of his title of Grand Secretary.

Below are all of Laurence Dermott's original notes, integrated from several editions of the text, with minor additions by the editor.

1. Quere, Whether such Histories are of any Use in the secret Mysteries of the Craft.
2. Next after the Title at the head of every chapter (except the ninth) of the Alcoran, is prefixed the following solemn form: *In the Name of the most merciful God.* [Alcoran is an obsolete Latinized reference to the name of the holy book of Islam, *al-Kuran.*— Ed.]
3. See Paradise Lost.
4. Fequin is supposed to be 7272 Miles East of London.
5. 1 Chron. ix.17.
6. See *Solomon's Temple Spiritualized* by Bunyan.
7. Jerusalem is supposed to be 2352 Miles S. E. by E. of London.
8. Flavius Josephus, the learned and warlike Jew. [This note was not in the original 1756 edition, nor the 1764 second edition, but appeared in some later printings. — Ed.]
9. Ezekiel.
10. Ezra.
11. Such was the Breast-Plate, worn by the High-Priest at the Temple. [This note was not in the original 1756 edition, nor the 1764 second edition, but appeared in some later printings. — Ed.]
12. Eccles. vi. 33, 34. [Notes 12 and 14 refer to Ecclesiasticus, a book in the apocrypha also known as the Wisdom of Ben Sirach. But in the final note, the *same* abbreviation is used to refer to a different book, Ecclesiastes, a part of the Hebrew Bible. — Ed.]
13. People skilled in the Cabala, *i.e.* Tradition, their secret Science of expounding divine Mysteries, &c.
14. Eccles. xxxii.1, 2, 3. [See note 12. — Ed.]
15. Eccles. ix. 8. [See note 12. — Ed.]

Before Dawn · *Shawn Eyer*

> When one obtains true knowledge, it is
> as though the Temple was built in his
> lifetime.
>
> Talmud, *Sanhedrin* 92a

Brethren, rouse yourselves,
For the sky lightens over our starlit quarries.
Dew-soaked tools, left without care in the
    moonlight,
Call for skilled hands,
Demand the dignity of use,
The nobility of honest work.

High on the hill, dear brethren,
Lies the holy Temple incomplete—
    but it shall not always be so.
For here where our fathers labored,
    now shall we,
Here in these ancient quarries,
    where in sacred memory
    strolled our prophets and our kings.

This must be the quietest place on earth.
But as God lives, let us put an end to this hush
And replace it with the clatter of work,
Let the distant towns hear
A great clamor from our ancient pits,
Let there be no question that again
    men and masons are at the stone.

Gleaming sun, rise! Dry our tools,
Warm our hands, illuminate our plans,
    and we will break the quietude of the night
Against the heat and tumult of noon!

There will be a place for silence,
A place where the only sound
Is the most mysterious word any man knows,
Whispered by one whose purpose from birth
    is to whisper it.

But we are not that man,
Hard work and noise are our lot,
And let us embrace it!

For you must understand
That we are builders,
And we are here to fashion fine stones,
And everything we need to work is here,
And we cannot be stopped from raising
    what we came here to erect.

2004

Ὀρθὴ δ' οὐκ ἐπιδέχεται σύγκρισιν οὐδ' ὀρθοτέρα γίνεται παρ' ἑτέραν, ἀλλ' ἐν ὁμοίῳ μένει τὴν ἰδίαν φύσιν οὔποτ' ἀλλάττουσα.

"The right angle does not entertain comparison, nor can any particular one of them be more accurate than any other, but each stands fast the same, its distinct nature ever unbending."

PHILO OF ALEXANDRIA

On the Creation of the World § 97

An Angle of Perfect Sincerity

Shawn Eyer

A T THE BANQUET set rich with game and foaming wine, surrounded by his admirers, reclined the great champion of the chariot races: Scopas, the son of Creon. His fame ever rising, his honors ever increasing, the young hero reveled in his own glory. Though in character he was base and of questionable morals, this seemed no detriment to the festivities, and as the night proceeded the irresistable delights of the fine food, the eloquent toasts, and the unrestrained adulation of his countrymen filled his senses with pride.

Also at table reclined worthy Simonides, an inspired poet of the island of Keos. Hired by Scopas to sing his praises, the bard was prepared with a fine song in tribute to the young champion and to the gods as well. The raucous hall quieted for his song, and he intoned the doings of Scopas alongside praises of Castor and Pollux, the sons of Zeus. He sang of great doings, noble victories, and hard questions:

'It is'—indeed, as the proverb says—
'hard for a man to become truly good,'
Foursquare in hand, foot and mind,
formed without a flaw.
No, this saying of the poet [Pittacus] is off-key,
however wise he may have been.
He said, it's hard to be truly good.
I say, only a god can own *that* state:
Man is base unavoidably.
In fair times he is fair,
When luck goes rotten so does he—
Even the nobility, whom the gods have so favored,
Fall under this rule, more or less.
So why should I search for the impossible,
Wasting the days of my life in an empty hope
To find a man without a flaw
Among us who are tilling the fields of
 this world?

If I do find him, I'll send word around,
But for now I'll praise and love one and all
Whose acts are base through no intention of
    theirs,
For not even the gods resist necessity itself.[1]

But when the final note was sung, the poet's ungallant host mocked him on the spot. "Only a third of the song was about me," complained Scopas, "so here is one-third of your fee. Perhaps Castor and Pollux will be happy to pay the rest of your charge." This outrageous insult fell easily from the tongue of the proud athlete, who was well aware that his cheated guest was from an island that stressed restraint in all things. Though mocked before the multitude, Scopas knew the poet would not make a scene.

It wasn't long after that a servant tapped Simonides, alerting him that two young men were outside and wanted to speak with him urgently. In the translation of our Brother Christopher Smart (the "Bedlam Poet"), Phædrus records that no sooner had the messenger

Roused from his seat the feasting bard,
Who scarce had stirred a single yard
Before the room at once fell in,
And crushed the champion and his kin.[2]

And thus the heaven-born twins paid Simonides their due for his hymn, even as the profane existence of Scopas was extinguished forever.[3]

This tale was repeated by many ancient authors, who probably saw in it a particularly acute illustration of *hubris*. *Hubris* was not, as we are commonly misinformed, a mere excess of pride. Aristotle says that the defining characteristic of *hubris* is

to cause shame to the victim, not in order that

anything may happen to you [for your benefit], nor because anything has happened to you [to your detriment], but merely for your own gratification. *Hubris* is not the requital of past injuries; that would just be revenge. As for the pleasure in hubris, its cause is that some men believe that by treating others improperly they somehow make their own superiority increase.[4]

Surely our legend of the poet and his ungrateful host offers a textbook example of hubris. But I propose that we embark upon a deeper analysis of the story—one that takes into account the perspective suggested by those who believe that myths describe conditions and conflicts within our own minds. Rather than see this as a simple tale of a good person who was insulted and a bad person who got a full dose of instant justice, let us consider this text from a more sophisticated point of view.

Aren't we all both Simonides and Scopas?

It might be easiest to think of ourselves as Simonides: talented, modest, and lucky to boot. Furthermore, we've all been cheated in some financial deal. We've all been mocked by someone. Psychologically and symbolically, Simonides represents our conscience, that voice of reality that (even in the midst of our neurotic denial) dares to *say something*. He's not the pure conscience, perhaps. He makes excuses and rationalizations about how hard it is to be good. But nevertheless he does speak the truth, when nobody else will. Who would not want to identify with Simonides?

But we must also own our Scopas within. Who hasn't felt the glow of fulfillment that comes from the adulation of peers when we are praised for some accomplishment, that healthy sense of pride that can turn—so easily, so subtly—into an unjustifiable derision for others, and an irrational sense of entitlement? And haven't we all been irritated by being reminded, however gently, that we need to make amends? We may imagine that we gain something by cheating our inner poet, whether it be a few silver coins or some ephemeral social status. And when building the walls of our spiritual house, who among us has raised every wall in perfect balance with the others—plumb, square and level—and composed only of stones connected exclusively by means of that blameless mortar recommended by our Craft?

Freemasonry acknowledges our inner Scopas in many ways. In the Mosaic Pavement. In the symbols of philosophical darkness, such as the hoodwink and the penal signs. And in the prayer we use at the opening of the Lodge, that we may "so subdue every discordant passion within us." The Craft has absolutely no illusions about purity coming to us easily. Nor does it fall under the error of an equally irrational cynicism that would consider our ideals unreachable and give up on them.

Within us too is the song of that ancient poet. It's hard to be truly good. Perhaps only the gods can be good, and it's okay to be imperfect. The trouble is not so much in the song as in our reaction to it. The song is quite true: it is hard, very hard to be truly and consistently good! But this fact can either inspire us to strive harder to be better men, or it can be used to rationalize away our failings—even, ultimately, to justify a cynicism that would convince us that it is useless to pursue a virtuous life.

As to the question of which perspective Simonides intended, it's interesting to note that this was debated centuries ago in Plato's dialogue, *Protagoras*.[5] And each of us continues that debate today, deep within ourselves, when we consider how committed we are, and how committed we ought to be, to our ideals.

Finally, we should ask what the symbolism might be of the two youths who sent the servant to tap on Simonides' shoulder. One could choose to understand this part of the legend as referring to the voice of intuition and instinct—a voice perhaps irrational, but no less real. Who hasn't regretted not following his instinct at times? And who hasn't felt that incredible relief that comes after following an instinct when it saves one from a bad situation?

So you may well see why I say that this ancient feast that went so wrong is also a fable that plays out constantly in our own hearts and in our own relationships. The message of this legend and the personal moral challenge that it represents is consonant with the teachings and values of Freemasonry.

In fact, an early version of the degree lectures published in 1775 by William Meeson actually quotes Simonides' poem, and Aristotle's discussion of its meaning:

> It was asserted by Aristotle, "that he who bears the shocks of fortune valiantly, and demeans himself uprightly, is truly good, and of a square posture without reproof." Now he that would smooth himself into such a perfect square posture, should often try himself by the perfect Square of justice and equality.[6]

Here the moral science of Freemasonry is at work, because we recognize that the "perfect square posture" is not a static condition, but one which must be aspired to by the constant application of the symbolic Square. Meeson's lecture defines the Square as "the theory of universal duty, [which] consisteth of two right lines, forming an angle of perfect sincerity, or ninety degrees."[7]

Brother Meeson's selection of this passage is particularly fitting, and it is almost a shame that his splendid bit of instruction faded from view after the Prestonian and Emulation lectures became dominant.

The image of the ἀνὴρ τετράγωνος, "the four-square man," is deeply evocative. Although the *hands* and *feet* are mentioned, they are invoked as the active extensions of a *four-square mind*.

> THE SQUARE is the theory of universal duty, and consisteth of two right lines, forming an angle of perfect sincerity, or ninety degrees; the longest side is the sum of the lengths of the several duties we owe to the Supreme Being; the other is made up of the lengths of the several duties we owe to all men. And every man should be agreeable to this Square when perfectly finished.
>
> —William Meeson, 1775

As scholar Maurice Bowra points out:

> This may be a Pythagorean notion; for the Pythagoreans thought that the square was the perfect figure and the image of divinity, and Aristotle, who knew their doctrine, accepted the identification of the four-square man with the good man, because 'both are perfect'. The notion may also have derived some support from the concept of the four cardinal virtues…. This concept indeed said nothing about physi-

cal qualities except in so far as they are implied in courage, but it is not ultimately far removed from the Pythagorean belief….[8]

It is interesting to observe the extent to which this pair of our Masonic concepts are grounded in ancient tradition: both the notion of the Square as a symbol of absolute truth and ideal goodness, and the concept of the just man properly governed by four cardinal virtues. According to this understanding, a true philosopher is one who stands in balance among attributes which connect him to deeper knowledge. Indeed, Plato said that the four virtues are a "preliminary purification" for the pursuit of wisdom.[9]

Upon reflection, we notice that Masonic tradition teaches exactly the same concept—namely that moral reflection and improvement must be a prerequisite to the higher philosophical truths of the Craft. In a cheap, modern way, we sometimes boil this down to a simple requirement that Masons or applicants for degrees not have any felonies on their records—but this disenchanted perspective is far from the original design that made our Order great. In fact, the Craft is founded on goodness. To be good and true is the first lesson we are taught, and it is a lesson that never ends for anyone who takes this path seriously and practices it in his daily life.

It is often said, also from a modern perspective, that Masonry's sole purpose is moral improvement. However often Masons may say this, the Masonic tradition (the body of instruction presented in the rituals and lectures of regular Freemasonry) does not. Instead, Masonry represents moral improvement as a foundational discipline in the support of a still higher purpose. In the old lectures of William Preston, written not long after Meeson's lecture, the question is posed, "Why morals before science?" (This is in reference to the respective lessons of the first and second degrees.)

The answer: "Because the secrets of nature must be imparted to those only who are incapable of abusing them."[10]

One rightly detects a hint of the ominous in that statement. This is wisdom worthy of serious reflection. Perhaps in our own experiences, we have seen the damage — sometimes of the most grievous nature — wrought by those who have come to believe that the Craft is a merely intellectual enterprise which binds us under no behavioral obligation. As Brother Wilmshurst reminds us, "Merely to know certain facts about the hidden side of life profits nothing unless the knowledge is allowed to influence and adapt our method of living to the truths disclosed."[11]

As the rough ashlars that we all assuredly are, we may have a tendency to grasp at higher truths while we have not yet established a firm enough foundation in our hearts and minds. This is not entirely a blameful thing — it's Promethean and heroic to surge ahead impetuously, and it may lead to flashes of higher knowledge far out of reach, though perceptable and thrilling. Before those insights can be truly ours, however, we will need to mold our lives to receive them.

But there is a point where rashness becomes hubris, and the profane, though drawn to the sacred, suffers by means of a careless intimacy with the holy. We learn in the *Sefer haZohar* that when the High Priest would enter the Temple to sprinkle the sacrificial blood in the Holy of Holies, a cord was tied around his ankle, should he lose in life in the innermost chamber—for a single impure thought while standing in the presence of G–d would be the death of him.[12]

While nothing so dramatic is likely to happen in a Masonic Temple, there are many kinds of destruction. As Brother Wilmshurst explains, the ill-prepared and unethical will make no true progress in the real work of Freemasonry, and ultimately will only harm themselves:

The depths of human nature and self knowledge, the hidden mysteries of the soul of man are not… probed into with impunity except by the "properly prepared." The man who does so has, as it

> THE SQUARE was the figure under which the Israelites formed their encampments in the wilderness, and under which they fortified or defended the holy tabernacle, sanctified with the immediate presence of the Divinity.
> —William Hutchinson, 1775

were, a cable-tow around his neck; because when once stirred by a genuine desire for the higher knowledge that real initiation is intended to confer, he can never turn back on what he learns thereof without committing moral suicide… And as the angel stood with a flaming sword at the entrance of Eden to guard the way to the Tree of Life, so will [a] man… find himself threatened at the door of the higher knowledge by opposing invisible forces if he rashly rushes forward in a state of moral unfitness into the deep secrets of the center. Better remain ignorant than embark upon this unknown sea unwisely and without being properly prepared and in possession of the proper passports.[13]

The surest way — the only way — to progress properly in our ancient and royal Art is to begin with a firm foundation. In the northeast corner of the lodge, where we were all placed, and where a part of us still stands looking upward to the East, we were told that we there stood just and upright, and it was given to us strictly in charge ever to walk and act as such. Masonry recognizes that we are all a mixture of light and darkness, and it acknowledges like the ancient poet that it is hard, sorrowfully hard, to be truly good. Even so, though we live in a world that responds to that difficulty with indifference and amorality, Freemasonry's perfect ashlar dares to call us to a higher ideal, an ancient humanistic notion of the ἀνὴρ τετράγωνος, the man "four-square in hand, foot and mind, formed without reproach." To walk that path we must continually "square our actions by the square of virtue," that is, in reference to the true, ultimate, divine nature of man.

Let us firmly resolve never to force that Square somehow away from the only "angle of perfect sincerity," for without that universal standard we will become unfit to try our stones, unable to remain objective in the face of our own rationalizations, and unworthy to penetrate into the true sanctum of the Masonic mysteries. If our tools are warped by impure intentions, then much like proud Scopas, we shall find our house crashing down, for untempered mortar is no mortar at all, and uneven masonry cannot stand.

Though the process is long and not at all painless, the relentless testing of our ashlars will make us better men in all practical and speculative matters, and perhaps we will come to more consistently embody those ideals so fittingly expressed in our lectures. May sincerity and plain dealing distinguish us, and hypocrisy and deceit become unknown among us. Let us never again address the Great Architect absent-mindedly when we ask that every discordant passion within us be subdued. And let us join together as brethren in an unbreakable mutual support as we improve ourselves, our lodges, and our world. ✦

Notes

1. Simonides, fragment 4.1–21 (author's translation).
2. *Phaedrus* 20.43–46.
3. In addition to the poetic account as cited in the previous note, the story can be found found in Cicero, *De Oratore* 2.86.
4. Aristotle, *Rhetoric* 1378b.
5. Protagoras 339a–344b.
6. W. Meeson, *An Introduction to Free Masonry* (Birmingham, England: Baldwin, 1775). Meeson is quoting Aristotle's *Nicomachean Ethics* 1100b21–22. In further discussion of the Square's symbolism, Meeson warnedw that "there is no medium betwixt sincerity and dissimulation, so of consequence he that is not a sincere man must be a deceitful one, than which none can be more pernicious to such a society. […] And certainly those who make no conscience wilfully to defeat that good-natured confidence which they have caused to be reposed in them by any other, have undoubtedly rotten hearts, and a very large share of dissimulation, impudence, and imposture. It is possible that some such as these may value themselves on the Square; but let me ask, how do they look unless they stand upright in the building?"
7. Ibid.
8. Cecil Maurice Bowra, *Greek Lyric Poetry from Alcman to Simonides* (Cambridge: Oxford University Press, 1961), 327–28.
9. Plato, *Phædo* 69A.
10. P. R. James, "The Second Lecture of Free Masonry by William Preston," *Ars Quatuor Coronatorum* 83(1970), 208.
11. W. L. Wilmshurst, *The Meaning of Masonry*. Rev. ed. (San Francisco: Plumbstone, 2007), 144–45.
12. Zohar 3.102a.
13. Wilmshurst, *Meaning of Masonry*, 59.

"In just the way that every marble block contains an unfinished statue as striking as the divine Apollo that was carved by Praxiteles, so each and every man bears within himself the human ideal."

Bro∴ José Martí

"Geometry, Divine Geometry, is the soul of the Craft, the model and sovereign adjuster of all its branches."

Bro∴ Hosea Ballou

1808

The Geometry of Character

Joseph Fort Newton

> And thus was the syence grounded there, and that worthy Mr. Euclid gave it the name of Geometrie, and now it is called through all this land Masonry.
>
> DOWLAND'S MS.

> These seven liberall Sciences are found under Geometry. Neither grammar, rhetorick, logick, nor any other of the said sciences can subsist without Geometry.
>
> HARLEIAN MS.

THE Old Charges speak of Geometry as the first of the sciences and the basis of the Masonic art. Of course, we do not have to accept the fantastic history which they relate as to the origin of Geometry. It is a tissue of legends, as interesting as they are impossible, in which Euclid is said to have been a close kinsman of Abraham! But it requires little insight to discern behind the rather crude records of the old documents of the Craft a memory, if nothing more, of the service of Geometry first to the physical and then to the spiritual life of man.[1]

In the Old Charges, as in our Ritual, we read of Pythagoras, who was the first thinker to raise mathematics to the level of a Divine Science, making it the foundation of a mystical philosophy. He held that Arithmetic is number at rest, while Music is number in motion. These formed the found liberal arts in his system. In the thought of Pythagoras, God was "the Great Geometrician," and in his hidden schools in Greece he taught his pupils that "all things are in numbers." He was concerned, as Proclus tells us, only with number and magnitude—in short, with mathematics and music.

Plato, following the path of Pythagoras, added three other arts, Grammar, Rhetoric, and Logic; and if a man knew these seven subjects he was held to be a man of learning. Plato, too, based everything upon numbers. Over the portal of his Academy in Athens he wrote the words: "Let no one who is ignorant of Geometry enter my doors." For him Geometry was a revelation of the Eternal Mind, a path to the knowledge of God, and as such a sacred and profoundly important art.

"What does the Deity do all the while?" one of his pupils asked.

"God is always geometrizing," was his reply. With which agrees his other famous saying: "Geometry must ever tend to draw the soul towards the truth." That is to say, what all the sciences are to our modern thinking—unveiling a world

> IT REQUIRES little insight to discern behind the rather crude records of the old documents of the Craft a memory, if nothing more, of the service of Geometry first to the physical and then to the spiritual life of man.

of law, order, and beauty—mathematics was to the early thinkers; and it is not strange that they regarded it with reverence and awe.

Three hundred years before our era, Euclid wrote his treatise in which he recorded all that was known of Geometry in his time; and his work still stands as the basis of the art of numbers. Better methods of proving problems have been developed, and new propositions have been discovered, but his initial insight is still valid. During the Dark Ages the science of Geometry was lost, along with much else of grace and value, in the inundation which buried classic culture; and men felt again the terror of chance, as primitive man had felt it long before. The rediscovery of Geometry by Simon Grynaceus, in the days of Luther, paved the way for modern science, and it no doubt had its influence on the documents of Masonry.

II

It is perhaps impossible for us at this distance to realize the service of the Science of Numbers to the faith and thought of man in his early thinking. It was almost his first hint of law and order in life when he sought to find some key to the mighty maze of things. Living in the midst of change and seeming chance, at the mercy of forces he did not understand, he found in the laws of numbers a path by which to escape from the awful sense of caprice and whim. Where there is no order, no stability, life hangs in the air, incalculable and terrifying. No wonder an art which revealed glimpses of unity and order in the world was held to be a Divine disclosure, and imparted its form to human faith. "Cannot the problems be made simpler?" King Ptolemy asked, after Euclid had shown him his treatise on Geometry. "There is no royal road to Geometry," the mathematician replied.[2]

True enough, as we learned in days gone by when we pondered over its problems; but Geometry itself became a royal road by which men discovered that Nature has certain attributes—First Truths, as they may be called—which lie at the foundation of all reasoning and research, and which may be assumed and acted upon with confidence.

By following the laws of numbers men learned to trace the regular motions of the heavens, the periodicity of the seasons, as well as to measure the earth—as in the valley of the Nile, Geometry was used to find the lines and landmarks erased by the annual inundation. So, naturally, as numbers had won order out of the chaos of their earliest impressions and misgivings, men exalted mathematics to the level of Divinity, as an inspiration of God. So, also, triangles and squares were engraved on their monuments and hung in their temples.

Having revealed so much, numbers naturally came to wear spiritual meanings, in a way quite alien to our prosaic way of thinking. No doubt that was what Plato meant when he said that by measurement the soul is saved—meaning that by ordering our lives in harmony with the eternal order of the world we are redeemed from futility. Hints of this science of numbers are found in the Bible, in which certain sacred numbers recur, indicating words, suggesting thoughts, revealing truths. The last book in the Bible, instead of being a series of clouded and confused visions, is in fact a book of spiritual mathematics. Three is the signature of Deity; Four indicates the world of created things; Seven denotes peace and covenant; Ten, completeness. Even numbers symbolize earthly things, odd numbers heavenly things; and the odd and even added unite the two—as they are united in the vision of the City of God, "according to the measure of man, that is, of the angel."

It is easy enough to say that such musings are mere fancies, but that is not so. To me one of the most impressive facts in the history of human thought is the way in which the first, fresh, creative ideas of the earliest thinkers have been confirmed by the research and experience of the race.[3]

For example, when Pythagoras said, "All things are in numbers; the world is a living arithmetic in development—a realized Geometry in repose," it was a daring insight of pure genius. Today we know that it is literally true. Take a snowflake and look at it under a magnifying glass, and you see as a fact what that mighty thinker saw as a vision. It is an exquisite example of the Geometry of God—squares, circles, triangles, pentagons, hexagons, parallelograms, more exact than the deftest hand could trace. Then look at the chart of an astronomer, and you will see writ in large letters in the sky what you read in small print in the snowflake. A dew-drop and a star are fashioned in the same way, and are ruled by the same laws.

Truly, God is always geometrizing, as Plato said; and these signs and designs, everywhere present in nature, must be the thoughtforms of the Eternal Mind, else they would not be the self-sought forms of matter and motion. Ages ago

> AS EUCLID had a mind deep enough and clear enough to discern and give first, if not final, expression to the laws of physical Geometry, so Moses, and the mighty moral seers, had minds lucid enough to discern a moral order.

Socrates tried to show Aristodemus, the Atheist, that as a statue by Polytectetus could not emerge from the quarries by mere chance, no more is it possible to imagine that the world—vaster and infinitely more intricate—came into being by chance. We take up a book like *The Life of the Spider* by Henri Fabre, and read these words, which would be understood by Pythagoras:

Geometry, that is to say, the science of harmony in space, presides over everything. We find it in the arrangement of a fir-cone, as in the arrangement of an Epeira's living web; we find it in the spiral of a snail shell, in the chaplet of a spider's thread, and in the orbit of a planet: it is everywhere, as perfect in the world of atoms as in the world of immensities. And this universal geometry tells us of a Universal Geometrician, whose divine compass has measured all things.[4]

Is it the ideal of a supreme Lover of Beauty, which would explain everything? Why all this regularity in the curve of the petals of a flower? Is that infinite grace, even in the tiniest details, compatible with the brutality of uncontrolled forces? One might as well attribute the artist's exquisite medallion to the steam-hammer which makes the slag sweat in the melting.

III

YES, God is always geometrizing—in the making of a man no less than the making of mountains and stars; in the fashioning of character as in the weaving of a spider's web. In other words, as Euclid had a mind deep enough and clear enough to discern and give first, if not final, expression to the laws of physical Geometry, so Moses, and the mighty moral seers, had minds lucid enough to discern a moral order. Nay, more; as in the mind of Euclid one attribute of the universe was made manifest, and in the moral insight of Moses another, so in the mind of Jesus—deep, sane, lucid, pure—the laws of the life of the spirit were most clearly revealed, and found their most perfect expression in His words.

These are but three forms of Geometry, physical, moral, and spiritual; and in each realm the vision is valid—moral and spiritual laws being as universal, as inescapable, as the laws of physics. Every movement of matter appears to conform to and be controlled by the laws and principles of mathematics. Not an atom curves anywhere in the universe that does not obey Geometry. When life entered, when mind and moral experience emerged, a new fact, a new force appeared, but the eternal laws ruled it. What we call spiritual values were revealed—truth, beauty, goodness, dedication, sacrifice. The universe produced these precious things as certainly as it produced pig-iron and potash—which means that it is a moral

and spiritual, as well as a physical, universe. The laws and principles of Geometry which control the forms and movements of matter are laws of our own minds, inevitable principles by which we do our thinking and living. In *Sermons of a Chemist* by E. E. Slosson, a man of science and a man of the spirit, there is a chapter entitled "The Geometry of Ethics," in which are these words:

Truth is one; falsehoods are infinite. Nine-tenths of the ideas that come into our heads are wrong. The object of education is to select the one that is right. Nine-tenths of the impulses that beset us are wrong. The task of civilization is to suppress the nine.

No matter how complex the problem, there is never more than one right answer, one right way out, one straight and narrow path, hard to find and hard to follow, one road leading out of the maze of many false turns; all the others are blind alleys or paths that return upon themselves. It is an axiom of plane geometry that there can be only one straight line connecting two points. From the point where we are to the point where we wish to go, there is only one straight road; all other possible paths are more or less divergent and devious.

The rules of conduct are as invariable and absolute as the rules of geometry. The only difference is that we cannot see so clearly in ethics as in mathematics. The falling of a fog makes our road obscure, but does not alter its length or direction. There is only one best move in a game of chess, whether we know what it is or not. There is only one wisest action in any emergency, whether we know what it is or not.[5]

Such is the kind of world in which we are set to find our way—an honest world in which law rules. Nothing moves haphazardly: in atom and star Geometry reigns, by the will of the Eternal Geometrician. No wildest comet goes flying through space but obeys the laws of numbers. Truly did the Psalmist say of old, "He hath set His compass upon the face of the deep." (Proverbs 8:27) Fortuitousness is a fiction. The laws of Geometry hold as true in the arts of man as in the art of God. A building is a geometrical demonstration. Painting is colored mathematics. Music is Geometry that has found wings and a voice. A good life is a geometrical life, fashioned by laws as universal as the laws of numbers.

IV

Emerson said in a great address that "the main enterprise of the world for splendor, for extent, is the upbuilding a man"—and that is the purpose of Masonry. As an old English Ritual tells us, "Geometry, or Masonry, originally synonymous terms, is of a divine and moral nature, and enriches the student with the most useful knowledge, and, whilst it proves the wonderful properties of Nature, demonstrates the more important truths of Morality." If we wish to put it so, Masonry is moral Geometry, and all its teaching rests upon the truth that the inner life of man—the life of faith, hope, duty, love—is a realm of law, where liberty and power and beauty are the trophies of faithful obedience and disciplined effort.

To put it plainly, order holds in the innermost places of the soul as much as in the heavens where the astronomer thinks the thoughts of God after Him. Character is no chance product, but is built according to laws as immutable and ascertainable as any law to be found in the laboratory. Freedom of soul is not capriciousness, least of all, lawlessness, but voluntary obedience to fixed laws of mind and spirit. He who builds according to the principles of righteousness will erect a character as stable as the house which the wise man built upon a rock. Storms do not shake it, floods do not undermine it. Happy is the man—memorable is the day for a young man—when he learns the Geometry of the heart, and vows to square his thought and action by the laws of the moral life, as he is taught in every lecture and obligation of his Lodge.

Let us consider, in a brief and vivid manner, the Geometry of character, its proportions and dimensions.

Like the City of God which the Seer saw descending from heaven, it is foursquare, its length and breadth and height equal. The basis of the cube of character—that is to say, the length of a

man, the extent of his influence and worth—is a matter of simple morality.

Purity is the first measure of a man. Lacking a certain sturdy moral quality—truthfulness, honor, cleanness—he is a man only by accident of his shape, though he have the learning of Bacon, the grace of Chesterfield, and the eloquence of Web-

> THERE IS YET another dimension of manhood, so often forgotten today, which we may call by the old word *piety*. It is a natural, normal development of man, without which his life lacks its crown, and is a thing unfinished.

ster. Morals are the boundaries of liberty and the primary fact of manhood. Nothing can take their place, since without a real moral life Religion is either a superstition or a sham. Morality is the foundation of character as it is the First Degree of Masonry.

But morality is not enough; a man may be both moral and mean—clean but cruel, righteous but uncharitable, truthful but narrow, honest but hard. If there is anything worse than the wrongs wrought by wicked men, it is the evil done by good men. That which gives breadth, beauty and mellowness to life, melting morality into goodness, is sympathy; and so to purity we must add pity. Justice runs lengthwise of life, but mercy is width, and is an evidence of nobility, of refinement, of graciousness of spirit. Lacking it, we have a Calvin in the Church consenting to the death of Servitus because of a difference of dogma, and in

fiction a Javert pursuing like a sleuth hound the weary, tangled, sorrowful feet of Jean Valjean, in the Victor Hugo story. Out of sympathy grows not only toleration, but understanding and appreciation—like a precious ointment healing the hurt and hardness of humanity. No one can forget how this is taught us in the Rite of Destitution, in the First Degree of Masonry.

In the Second Degree we are urged to use and develop our power of mind, by such study of the arts and sciences as may "lie within the compass of our attainment"—a necessary qualification, as otherwise it would set a task outside the range of human possibility. It is an exhortation to that intellectual culture without which manhood is rudimentary, a challenge to seek what Emerson called "the great freedoms of the mind," whereby we are lifted above narrowness and prejudice. It invites us to breadth of view, balance of judgment, and beauty of mind made rich by the treasures of truth stored up for our use and joy. To purity and mercy must be added "the moral obligation to be intelligent," skillful, and wise. Clear thinking is as much a duty as kindness of heart. A noble sincerity may be dangerous if devoted to error and unwisdom, and as much a deformity as the mind of a philosopher attached to the appetite of a pig. Both betray a lack of symmetry, a flaw in the art of life.

There is yet another dimension of manhood, so often forgotten today, which we may call by the old word PIETY. Some, to be sure, think it a kind of fourth dimension, a thing which you may argue exists, but which we can never realize. Not so. It is a natural, normal development of man, without which his life lacks its crown, and is a thing unfinished. Man must be tall of soul as well as broad, if he is to see life in the large, much less "see it steadily and see it whole," as the wise ones enjoin us to do. Altitude of mind gives us new proportions and perspectives, and shows us that many things of which men are wont to make much are insignificant; and that other things, like a cup of cold water offered to a brother, are of eternal moment.

It is when we add this dimension that we see what man really is, measured by what is immeasurable in him. In how many ways Masonry appeals to these "better angels of our nature," seeking to evoke that within us akin to the Eternal, and which can only be uttered in symbol and sanctity and song!

Such is the spiritual Geometry of Masonry; and upon this earth there is nothing finer or more precious than the quality of character which it creates. Our kindly earth, with its swiftly flowing nights and days, knows nothing greater than a great life, founded upon moral worth, lighted by the truth, warmed by a gentle fraternal spirit, touched to tenderness by the beauty and pathos of mortal things, busy in the service of the best causes, erect, unafraid, reverent, happy, faithful—it is the consummation of all the world, and a bright star in the glory of God.

V

In the symbolism of all peoples, in the dream of all seers, there is a vision of a Temple, of which the Temple on Mount Moriah was a parable and prophecy, slowly rising without the sound of hammer or chisel, a "Temple not made with hands, eternal in the heavens." (2 Corinthians 5:1) Into that Home of all Souls, at once a shrine of faith and a shelter of the holy things of life, each of our lives is builded as living stones, by the same laws of moral Geometry. So that whatever immortality of worth or beauty may be won out of our piteous, passionate and prophetic life on earth, will be shared by all who sought the truth and served the will of God in purity of heart and fidelity of purpose.

There, on the Trestle-Board, is the plan of the Great Architect, and our business is to build together by the light of the ideal shown us in the Book of Holy Law. Out of the rough and noisy quarries of the world we are to bring the stones, polished and finely wrought, and build a Temple of Faith and Friendship, of Brotherhood and Truth. The Temple is the great Landmark—the great aim and ideal of Masonry. To build, to strengthen, to beautify it is our duty and dream, each one adding a stone to its loveliness. Nobler work is not given man to do. Happy is he who, as a faithful craftsman of the soul, can say in truth at the end of the day, "Thank God, I have marked well." ⨎

Notes

1. It is not the purpose of these pages to expound in detail the religious suggestions of the symbolism of Masonry—that task must wait. Elsewhere, in a little book entitled *Brothers and Builders*—published in America under the title *Degrees and Great Symbols* in the Little Masonic Library—I have tried to interpret some of the major symbols of the Lodge. If half my dreams come true I hope to carry the study further, seeking to interpret the symbolism of the Craft in the context of universal symbolism, as hinted to us in such a book as *The Migration of Symbols*, by Count D'Alviella.

   Meanwhile, we have noble books in this field, such as *The Symbolism of Freemasonry*, by Mackey, *The Symbolism of the Three Degrees*, by O. D. Street, *Symbolical Masonry*, by H. L. Haywood, *Foreign Countries*, by Carl H. Claudy, *An Interpretation of Masonic Symbols*, by J. S. M. Ward; and of a more mystical kind the writings of Waite and Wilmshurst, especially *The Masonic Initiation*, the while we look forward to the lectures on symbolism by Dean Roscoe Pound, and particularly his lecture on "The Mysticism of Masonry."

2. The 47th Problem of Euclid served as the frontispiece of Anderson's *Constitutions*, issued in London in 1723, accompanied by the word

Eureka in Greek. In the text of the Constitutions the problem is declared to be, "if duly observed, the foundation of all Masonry, sacred, civil and military"—whatever that may mean. In the second edition of the *Constitutions*, in 1738, it is spoken of as that "amazing proposition which is the foundation of all Masonry, of whatever materials and dimensions." After that it is rather tame to read in our ritual that "it teaches us to be general lovers of the arts and sciences." No wonder Speth remarked that "while our medieval Brethren may have been familiar with its symbolic meaning, we are not."

What did Pythagoras mean by the Great Symbol? Evidently the symbolism was not in the figure but in the numbers three, four, five—especially three and four, the sum of which make the sacred number Seven. Why was seven sacred? Seven what? Perhaps the seven Divine potencies of the theology of Median Magi, under whom he studied. Of the seven three were feminine and four masculine—the female powers forming the base of the right-angled triangle, the male forces the perpendicular; the two combining to make the *Father-Mother* God, the discovery of which was indeed a revelation! What may the problem mean to us? What, indeed, if not that the reality of God is revealed only to the total powers of man, the sum of his perceptive and receptive faculties—intuition and intellect, heart and reason; and that to find God in a satisfying manner requires the fusion of all our powers of thought, will, action, love in a mystical experience—whereof our Ritual is a dim and faded shadow for most Masons!

3. At the same time we ought to remember that the universe, as science reveals it, is a very different universe from anything the early thinkers imagined. The universe as seen by geometry is not unlike what William James called a "block universe," whereas the real universe is a living universe, not so much a mechanism as an organism. Science knows nothing of "dead matter," in the old sense of the word; indeed, it does not know what it is at all, except that it is alive with energy. Anyway, the universe in which Einstein works is very unlike the universe in which Isaac Newton lived and wrought. If any reader wishes a popular discussion of the matter, he may find it in *A Living Universe* by L. P. Jacks, a most delightful and inspiring book, seeking to interpret the new universe—new to us—in which we live in spiritual terms. The laws and truths of geometry remain, only it is a living geometry—living laws, not dead rules—as Masonry should be. If Masonry is "a progressive science," as we read in the Ritual, it must take account of the swiftly changing vision of the universe, and interpret its teaching accordingly. Indeed, one sometimes wishes that a new Preston might arise and use Masonry as a means of teaching the truth about the world as we now know it through science, as the first Preston did in days of old.

4. Jean-Henri Fabre, *The Life of the Spider* (New York: Dodd, Mead & Co., 1915), 399–400.

5. Edwin E. Slosson, *Sermons of a Chemist* (New York: Harcourt, Brace & Co., 1925), 200–201.

Charge · *Gregory Maier*

Stone cutters, build not only for yourselves
and your ambitious yearnings,
challenging oblivion:
You are defeated
fighting time with marble
like the Greeks and Romans.

Beautiful and empty temples you may make,
the sepulchers of tomorrow.

For you will pass, reclaimed
even as your vaults rise, columns erected,
    corridors lengthened gathering the future's dust.

Remember your Brothers
and those to come
laboring athirst in the quarries,
as you have.

Build you also wells
that others may drink
And fashion living stones,
foundations of strength, and paths to guide
    intact
others who humbly journey to the portal of
    mystery.

Listen
to the silence in the stone
unfallen, unworn by rain:
Life — forever!

A Spiritual Vision of the Seven Liberal Arts

Thomas D. Worrel

> Wisdom builded her house;
> She has hewn out her seven pillars.
>
> Proverbs 9:1

> At your leisure hours you are required
> to study the liberal arts and sciences,
> and by that means, with a few private
> instructions, you will soon attain a
> competent knowledge of our mysteries.
>
> William Preston
> *Illustrations of Masonry*, 1775

ONE

The Winding Staircase
& the Seven Liberal Arts

ONE OF THE MOST impressive ceremonies of American Craft Freemasonry is the section of the second degree known as the "staircase lecture" or the "Middle Chamber lecture." This important part of our Masonic tradition covers many subjects pertinent to the mysteries of Freemasonry. These are presented through the explanations of the three, five and seven steps that compose the stairs. When the lecture arrives at the seven steps, the Fellow Craft is told little more than that they collectively represent the seven liberal arts and sciences. In some rituals, these are each briefly described. In many, however, the subjects are enumerated without detail, except for the art of geometry, which is always explained as the most important of the seven.

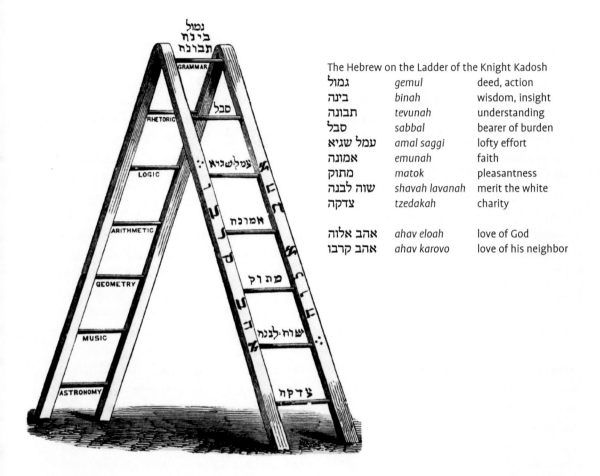

The Hebrew on the Ladder of the Knight Kadosh

גמול	gemul	deed, action
בינה	binah	wisdom, insight
תבונה	tevunah	understanding
סבל	sabbal	bearer of burden
עמל שגיא	amal saggi	lofty effort
אמונה	emunah	faith
מתוק	matok	pleasantness
שוה לבנה	shavah lavanah	merit the white
צדקה	tzedakah	charity
אהב אלוה	ahav eloah	love of God
אהב קרבו	ahav karovo	love of his neighbor

In this situation, we are left with more questions than answers. Why are these particular subjects mentioned? It is certainly debatable whether or not these are the most important academic disciplines. Why are there just seven? There are certainly more than just seven arts and sciences. Why are they in a staircase motif? If we took the staircase to represent levels of prerequisite education, or of understanding, or of importance, there would be considerable disagreement regarding this order. What we are really left with are the implications derived from the comments on geometry—that is, that these are subjects worthy of study and geometry is the most important of the seven. We are then left with the broadest question of them all: Is this the real message to the candidate?

Many have assumed that this part of the Masonic tradition is simply a vestigial remnant of the obvious reliance of the operative craft upon the science of geometry. Others may be inclined to interpret the Fellow Craft teachings about the seven liberal arts only as a vague message in favor of education generally. Either way, it is common for Freemasons to conclude that the arts and sciences refer to mundane disciplines and skills — subjectively bearing only on the material well-being and capability of man.

The history of the seven liberal arts tells us a completely different story. Their origin lies in classical antiquity, and their role in the development of Western civilization has been immense. Their adoption among the Fraternity suggests far more than currently realized. And because its history and relevance to both our culture and our Craft was so central, it highlights a problem in our Lodges today: what was once a precious adornment of our tradition has now become perceived as little more than a footnote in our second degree. I believe that the neglect of the study of these arts drains the life-blood from our august body. The purpose of this paper is to look at something we have lost; to try and reestablish our connection with a part of our past; and, in a broader sense, issue a call to preserve one of the true beauties within our fraternity of Freemasonry.

There are already many commentaries on the winding staircase by various Masonic writers. Usually the explanations of the seven liberal arts are somewhat vague. It is common to find rudimentary definitions of the seven subjects. Sometimes there is a little more elaboration but it often seems in complete. But, as we combine the different views, the Masonic significance becomes clearer.

The Interpretations of Masonic Authors

There are many Masonic writers who have considered the question of the seven liberal arts. Space permits mention of only a few, but these will provide at least a survey of the differing views. There is a common thread: most Masonic writers at least sense that the winding staircase is something more than it at first appears. From that point, the opinions seem to diverge into several different directions. As H. L. Haywood states in his book, *Symbolical Masonry*: "The Three, Five and Seven Steps have long been a puzzle to the candidate and a problem to Masonic writers…"[1]

While most writers correctly point out that the classification of the seven arts comes from the Medieval educational curriculum, the real question for Freemasons is not *where* it originated, but why is it included in our rites.

Haywood expresses a view that is widespread among Masonic writers:

I believe that Masonry is justified in retaining the Liberal Arts and Sciences in its Ritual just because they still have power to humanize us, to 'improve us in social intercourse,' to make us broader of mind, more tolerant in opinion, more humane in action, and more brotherly in conduct. Besides, knowledge of them…can make us more useful to the lodge.[2]

He goes on to explain how useful it is for a Lodge to have members who can write, play music, and speak. He seems to consider the seven arts as merely having useful educational purposes.

H.P. H. Bromwell (1823–1903) wrote in his massive tome *Restorations of Masonic Geometry and Symbolry* that "Although the number of recognized sciences far exceeds seven, yet, giving to that number the benefit of its symbolic meaning, it stands for the whole circle of sciences, whether specifically named among the seven or not."[3] Here is an example of someone who considers that the number seven is used in its symbolic sense of meaning "the whole picture" or "all encompassing". We can speculate that his interpretation is that the seven liberal arts refers to all knowledge.

In *Stellar Theology and Masonic Astronomy* Robert Hewitt Brown interprets just about everything in the ritual in an astronomical way:

The wages of the faithful craftsmen, we are told, are 'corn, oil and wine.' The seven signs of the zodiac, from the vernal equinox to the first point of Scorpio, 'winding' in a glittering curve about the heavens, may in a like manner be said to be emblematic of seven winding steps…thus corresponding with the more ancient versions of the fellow-craft legend…[4]

While this is an interesting point of view, it seems to completely ignore both the specific subjects of the seven steps, and the history of the curriculum.

There are Masonic authors who interpret the seven liberal arts in ways that are not based upon historical knowledge but in terms of psychology, philosophy or spirituality. W. Kirk MacNulty is a case in point:

> In the most general terms the winding staircase defines seven 'levels of consciousness', from consciousness of the physical body at the bottom to consciousness of the Spirit and Divinity at the top. By summarizing a large body of ritual and lecture, we can say that the Stairs assign a step or level of consciousness to each of the seven Officers of the Lodge…. [5]

His correspondences are the following: Tyler with Grammar, Inner Guard with Logic, Junior Deacon with Rhetoric, Senior Deacon with Arithmetic, Junior Warden with Geometry, Senior Warden with Music, and the Worshipful Master with Astronomy. This type of explanation deals more with how one might currently interpret the seven liberal arts but does not address the original intent of the founders of the Craft.

Another author in this survey is George H. Steinmetz. In his book *Freemasonry: Its Hidden Meaning* he also tackles the seven steps. He makes the cryptic statement: "…the seven steps have a deep occult meaning which we will merely mention here. They are the vibrations producing color and sound."[6] He does not elaborate on this, but a few pages later he

states: "There are actually seven interpretations of Masonic symbolism, or more correctly, seven means of interpretation."[7] He goes on to explain how each discipline can individually be applied to the rites of Freemasonry to garner ever deeper interpretations. There may be some truth here, although it is a clumsy fit with some of the disciplines. Certainly there is much in Masonic tradition of an astronomical nature, and much is related to geometrical and number symbolism. One can make some case for the others, but it begins to get weaker and weaker.

In the Scottish Rite's thirtieth degree, titled Knight Kadosh or Knight of the Holy Spirit, we again encounter the seven liberal arts. Here they are depicted on a double seven-runged ladder. Albert Pike's explanation in the *Liturgy* is really based around the lessons of the Knight Kadosh degree, but we get hints of a deeper and more mystical significance when we consider the corresponding words on the other side of the ladder whose seven rungs are labeled in Hebrew. It may a loose allusion to the *sefirot* (or "spheres") of kabbalah, the Jewish mystical tradition, which themselves form a "ladder" of sorts known as the *etz khayim* or Tree of Life.

Pike states in the *Legenda*: "[…I]n this Degree, the words on the seven steps of the Ladder mean something more and higher than the mere elementary Sciences of which they are the names."[8] Pike's commentary then explains these seven arts as steps to ever-larger vistas of God and Creation; and, with the corresponding rungs on the opposite side, develops a much more exalted role of these arts and sciences.

The last Masonic writer I wish to introduce is Walter Leslie Wilmshurst (1867–1939). He is the author of several books including *The Meaning of Masonry*, *The Masonic Initiation* and *The Ceremony of Passing*. Wilmshurst's perspective was unabashedly mystical:

The perambulations are made on the level floor of the Lodge, which the candidate keeps on "squaring," visiting each of its four sides in turn. But at the end of the third circuit the moment comes when his forward motion on the level ceases, and he is directed to mount spirally, by a series of winding steps. Linear motion gives way to circular; he advances now not merely forward, but up. … By this change of motion, this spiral ascent, is implied that the time has come when the Candidate must leave the level of the sense-world and rise to the supra-sensual; must divert his thoughts and desires from sensuous objects and concentrate them on the insensible and much more real things of the world of mind.[9]

Clearly, Wilmshurst is of the opinion that the winding staircase, which includes the seven steps, is considerably more than an exhortation on the merits of an extensive education. The winding stairs become the vehicle of his ascension into the spiritual realm.

From the moment of ascending the winding staircase, then, the Candidate is mentally leaving the outer world more and more behind him and rising into an inner invisible world. He is making what has often been called *Itinerarium mentis in Deo*, the ascent of the mind to the Source of Light…[10]

This short survey of Masonic writers' views shows the great diversity of opinion that exists on the topic of the winding staircase.

While some see the symbol in its most mundane interpretation, others consider it a vehicle to mystical heights. Exploring the seven liberal arts in a wider historical context will help us to develop our own view.

The Seven Liberal Arts Through the Centuries

The history of the seven liberal arts is the history of the development of education up until the end of the Middle Ages. Its origins are in classical Athens. The different disciplines were developing at different times and it was not until later that they crystallized into a set of seven. The term "liberal" has lead to some confusion because we use the term somewhat differently now. Today, we tend to connect it to a broad and eclectic education in contrast to a highly specialized technical or professional education. But "liberal," in the context of the seven liberal arts, means "suitable for free men." And the term "arts" has to be thought of in the sense of "skills."

The term *liberal arts* is used as early as Plato (428–348 BCE). Both Plato and his pupil Aristotle had a model curriculum, in which different subjects were stressed at different times. In the *Republic*, the quadrivium are treated as subjects to prepare for the highest type of knowledge. By the third century BCE, the curriculum often consisted of gymnastics, grammar, music, drawing, arithmetic and geometry. Other subjects often taught were medicine and architecture.

Later, the Romans adopted the Greek ideas of education. By the fourth century CE the pagan schools had fixed their curriculum to seven arts, an arrangement soon adopted by Christian thinkers. The first Christian to use the term "seven liberal arts" was Cassiodorus (480–575 CE).[11] This curriculum remained fixed throughout the Middle Ages. Its full flowering was exemplified by the Cathedral School at Chartres in the twelfth century.

These seven subjects — grammar, rhetoric, logic, arithmetic, geometry, music, and astronomy—were considered a unity. They were divided into two parts: the trivium of grammar, rhetoric and logic; and the quadrivium of arithmetic, geometry, music and astronomy. All seven formed an integrated whole which also made all seven necessary. And it must be remembered who put these subjects together. William Stahl explains that "the people who were most interested in the full span of subjects were philosophers; and the seven liberal arts were in essence, and always remained, a philosophers' curriculum."[12]

The study of *grammar* encompassed not only parts of speech and rules but also literature, reading, exposition, etymologies and what we now call linguistics. All instruction was in Latin; therefore, mastery of the Latin language was preliminary to everything else. *Rhetoric* is the training of the orator or developing the practice of speaking to the level of an art. But in the Latin West it took the forms of learning how to produce proper letters and documents. How to make appropriate addresses and petitions and so on. *Logic* was not so much as a preparation for philosophy but the study of formal logical methods. *Arithmetic* was basically the art of computation, but there was strong interest in its mystical and symbolic implications due to influence from the Pythagorean traditions. *Geometry* was not anything like we now conceive until the tenth century. It was not until the twelfth and thirteenth centuries that complete translations of Euclid from the Arabic were available. *Music* was completely theoretical: a mathematical and speculative science (a perspective traditionally traced to the Pythagoreans). *Astronomy* was very popular, as there was a great interest in all things pertaining to the heavens, including astrology.

It is well to keep in mind the intention of the schoolmasters in using this curriculum. This is best illustrated by the activities going on at the magnificent Gothic cathedral at Chartres in France in the twelfth century.

The Cathedral and School of Chartres

There is some evidence that, as early as the sixth century, Chartres was a center of learning. But it was not until the twelfth century that it became the center of Latin Platonism and a school where students flocked to learn the highest philosophy of the land.

The geographic area itself is interesting. There is a legend that it was once used by the Celtic druids as a sacred site. The cathedral also sits on a granite promontory that cuts through the limestone plain. This fact corresponds to the structure of Stonehenge where the concentric circles were hewn out of granite and set on the limestone of Salisbury Plain.[13]

The cathedral and school are important to us here because the seven liberal arts reached not only a high degree of perfection as taught but it seems that the architecture also gave witness to this same spirit. The seven liberal arts "as a means to the knowledge of God finds visible expression in the cathedral at Chartres."[14] Adolf Katzenellenbogen states in his work that:

If one studies the representations of the seven liberal arts in the twelfth century one realizes that they are only a link in the whole chain of representations of this subject, and that a long tradition of ideas and forms lies behind their images. [...] It is generally agreed that the first façade on which the seven arts were represented was that of the Royal Portal of Chartres Cathedral. [... T]hese systems of decoration indicate in different ways the relation of secular learning to theological truths."[15]

Thierry was chancellor of the School when the figures were carved. He was also in charge of supervising various parts of building the cathedral. One may readily perceive a tangible correlation between the final form of the architectural design and the philosophical conceptions of the designer. In Thierry's own handbook on the seven liberal arts, he defined the specific role of the Quadrivium as illuminating the mind and that of the Trivium as making its expression. Raymond Klibansky explains how Thierry's influence spread throughout Europe:

Under him Chartres became the center of the liberal arts to which students came from all over Europe. In search of new sources of knowledge, his pupils crossed the Pyrenees and the Alps. They brought back mathematical and astronomical works in translations made from the Arabic, and new texts of Aristotle in versions made from the Greek. From Chartres this new learning was handed on to the Latin world.[16]

It is true that the School laid emphasis on the Quadrivium, but Klibansky informs us that the purpose behind this was

to attain, through knowledge of the structure of the created world, knowledge of the Creator. As the world...is ordered according to number, measure, and weight, the sciences of the quadrivium — arithmetic and geometry, music and astronomy — are the instruments which the human mind has at its disposal for recognizing the art of the Creator.[17]

It was a grand school with grand designs, fully engaged in all of the classic liberal arts and sciences as part of a spiritual imperative to create a holy structure that would truly reflect the divine world, beautifully linking heaven and earth. As David Luscombe states:

> [...T]he Chartrains attempted to establish the existence of God by numerical speculations, to synthesize Platonic cosmology and biblical revelation, and to compare the Platonic world soul with the Holy Spirit...[and] God was considered to be the form of all being.[18]

TWO

The Art of Memory
and a Spiritual Vision of the Liberal Arts

The Winding Staircase
as a Symbol of Ascension

A full understanding of the seven liberal arts in a Masonic context must take into account its use as symbolism. The seven are actually contained within another symbol: the winding staircase. It is interesting and informative to look at how the symbol has been interpreted in psychological ways and also how it has been portrayed in religious art, story and legends.

The winding staircase is an image that refers to upward movement — of moving from one level to a higher level. Related images include ladders, mountains, towers, and the act of flight. We can also include the image of climbing a rope or a cosmic pillar — or in this modern time, taking an elevator. Jungian psychologist Edward F. Edinger classifies this type of image under the term *Sublimatio*. It is an alchemical term, and it may be that he retains the Latin spelling in order to distinguish the idea from the Freudian term "sublimation," which is not the same psychological mechanism. Freud uses "sublimation" to refer to the way we channel our animal instincts into socially acceptable behavior.

In alchemical tradition, *sublimatio* is the basic chemical operation of turning material into air by volatilizing it, it then turns into air and reformulates in a higher place. In a lab it works like this: take a certain solid; apply heat; it turns into gas; it ascends, then cools; then it resolidifies. Distillation is related, but is applied to liquids, such as when we heat water to boil, capture the steam, and it recondenses to water as it cools — leaving the heavy contaminants behind in the original vessel. According to Edinger:

> ...the crucial feature of *sublimatio* is an elevating process whereby a low substance is translated into a higher form by an ascending movement. [...] *Sublimatio* is an ascent that raises us above the confining entanglements of immedi-

ate earthly existence and its concrete, personal particulars.[19]

From the Jungian point of view, this process can take different forms. It can manifest as seeing a problem from a broader perspective: maybe something has troubled an individual to where his functioning in some area of his life is restricted, and then by some event or change his view of the situation completely alters and he sees it from a higher perspective which lessens its original hold upon him. Or even to the extreme event of some mystical experience which usually overturns ones life and washes away many of the petty things we once felt were so important; and consequently frees us — or volatizes our consciousness — where we can view things "from on high."

Edinger points out that many of the alchemical processes overlap. Overlapping with sublimation is the process of separation or *separatio*. They are both extraction processes. The "spirit" is extracted from "matter." Therefore, the ultimate sublimation is death which would remind us of the degree following the Fellow Craft. The alchemists sometimes referred to the spirit of man as quicksilver.

Edinger states that: "This 'expulsion of the quicksilver' is done by *sublimatio*, which releases the *spirit hidden in matter* [my emphasis]. In the largest sense, this refers psychologically to the redemption of the Self from its original unconscious state."[20]

This statement is also interesting in a kabbalistic sense in Freemasonry. The words *or ganuz* (אור גנוז) meaning "hidden light" have the same numerological value as Hiram Abiff: that is, 273.[21]

The situation as the alchemists saw it was that matter and spirit was intermixed in a basic state of contamination. Thus, the need for

the alchemical procedures of extraction. The procedures produced a purified state by separation. The seven liberal arts were thought of as achieving the same ends. It was considered a way of purifying the soul so that it could ascend to the spiritual realms. Another aspect of sublimation that Edinger mentions is the theme of translation to eternity. As examples, he relates the stories of ancient heroes being taken to the realms of the gods such as Heracles, Elijah, Christ and the Virgin Mary. We find this theme in ancient Egypt as well:

…the model of a ladder was often placed on or near the dead body in the tomb, and a special composition was prepared which had the effect of making the ladder become the means of the ascent of the deceased into heaven. Thus in the text written for Pepi the deceased is made to address the ladder in these words: "Homage to thee, O divine Ladder! Homage to thee, O Ladder of Set! Stand thou upright, O divine Ladder! Stand thou upright, O Ladder of Set! Stand thou upright, O Ladder of Horus, whereby Osiris came forth into heaven."[22]

The resurrected Osiris is sometimes pictured in Egyptian art as a ladder with arms holding the Crook and Scourge.

We find ladder and stair symbolism in many myths which are clear symbols of ascending and descending. The phenomenon is prevalent throughout the world. The historian of world religions, Mircea Eliade, comments in his book on shamanism that:

The pre-eminently shamanic technique is the passage from one cosmic region to another — from earth to the sky or from earth to the underworld. The shaman knows the mystery of the break-through in plane. This communica-

Mony eres aft ye goode clerk Euclyde
Taughte ye craft of gemet wond wyde
So he dede yt tyme oy al so
Of dyuers craftes mony mo
Throgh hye grace of crist yn heuen
He comensed yn ye syens seuen

tion among the cosmic zones is made possible by the very structure of the universe [.... which] is conceived as having three levels — sky, earth, underworld — connected by the central axis.[23]

Eliade mentions a few ancient mysteries and religious traditions that seem to parallel our Masonic tradition:

A ladder with seven rungs is documented in the Mithraic mysteries.... An ascent to heaven by ceremonially climbing a ladder probably formed part of the Orphic initiation.... the symbolism of ascension by means of stairs was known in Greece. [...] Jacob dreams of a ladder whose top reaches heaven.... Mohammed sees a ladder rising from the temple in Jerusalem to heaven.... in Islamic mysticism to ascend to God, the soul must mount seven successive steps.... In the heaven of Saturn Dante sees a golden ladder rising dizzyingly to the last celestial sphere and trodden by the souls of the blessed.[24]

These are only a few examples that could be given. A study of world mythology reveals this same motif all over the planet from the most "primitive" tribes to the most sophisticated cosmologies.

We can now see the powerful use that Freemasonry developed in the Fellow Craft degree as regards the seven liberal arts and the winding staircase. There is symbolism nested within symbolism. Not only do we have a symbol of ascending in that of the winding staircase, but also that of steps divided into three, five, and seven — all mystical numbers with their own significance. Corresponding with these seven steps are the seven liberal arts, and the mythic context of this ascent as a launching point of the mind to scale the realms of the Spirit.

It is my contention that the seven liberal arts were included in the Masonic ritual for a far greater purpose than secular educational

▲ A section from the Regius Poem, as preserved in the Halliwell Manuscript, circa 1400 CE. See the translation on page 45.

▶ An early printing of Martianus Capella's treatise *On the Marriage of Philology and Mercury*, which was the first appearance of the seven liberal arts as they are known in Freemasonry.

reasons. After all, their original purpose in classical antiquity was philosophical: their high purpose in the Latin West was as a preliminary study for theology. As such, they are featured prominently on the façade of the West portal of the Chartres Cathedral, a structure where the seven arts might be said to have reached their highest expression. In the same spirit, they are incorporated into the poetry of Dante Alighieri (1265–1321) and into the practices we call the "art of memory," including the use of the image of King Solomon's temple.

The formulation of the seven liberal arts began in classical antiquity. The quadrivium was taught as early as Plato. In the *Republic*, they are treated as subjects to prepare for the highest type of knowledge.[25] It was not until later that the subjects crystallized into the seven we call familiar. The curriculum of the seven liberal arts evolved from earlier Greek and then Roman systems of education. Scholars hold that the fourth century was when the seven arts became the standard curriculum of the pagan schools. It wasn't until later that it was modified to exhibit Christian ideals.

This was a century of transition. The nominally Christian Constantine the First became sole emperor in 324 CE. Sometime before 330, Martianus Capella, a pagan writer, wrote his book *De Nuptiis Philologiæ et Mercurii* (On the Marriage of Philology and Mercury), which preserved the basic structure of the ancient educational system based on the seven liberal arts. Later in that century, the imperial decree of Theodosius in 392 prohibited all pagan teachings. As a result, the sanctuaries were destroyed and the initiatic lines began to disappear. Rome was sacked by Alaric in 410. About nineteen years later the Vandals conquered North Africa. By 450, all the remaining pagan temples were being destroyed and non-Christians were banned from holding public office.

While Christian leaders were originally suspicious of the pagan philosophies, eventually

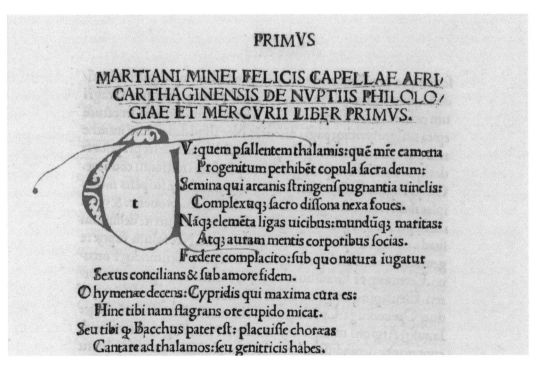

they began to incorporate elements of them. This curriculum was adopted and basically remained fixed throughout the Middle Ages—its ultimate expression taking form at the Cathedral School at Chartres in twelfth century France.

The Old Tales

Martianus Capella's treatise *The Marriage of Philology and Mercury* is the earliest depiction of the seven liberal arts as a unified course of study. Besides offering a description of the seven arts, it also tells an allegorical legend:

> Mercury, after some unsuccessful attempts to secure a suitable wife, consults Apollo, who advises him to marry Philology, an astonishingly erudite young lady. The suggestion meets with the approval of both parties, and Philology, after considerable preparation and instruction, is wafted to the upper heavens, where her marriage is to take place before a "Senate" consisting of gods, demigods, and philosophers. The connection between the setting and the seven liberal arts becomes clear when an elderly but attractive lady named Grammar, one of the seven learned sisters, is introduced to present her discipline first to the assembled wedding guests. The seven sisters, personifications of the seven disciplines, have commonly been referred to as bridesmaids. They are bridesmaids only in the broadest sense of the word, however. Martianus calls them *feminæ dotales* and, if we consider his fondness for legal vocabulary, the term should be translated as "ladies constituting a dowry." That is what they actually are: handmaids presented by Mercury to his bride. The marriage of Mercury and Philology has been taken, both early and late, to symbolize the union of eloquence and learning, the arts of the trivium and the quadrivium.[26]

About a thousand years later, Dante refers to the seven liberal arts in both his *Divine Comedy* (started in 1302) and in the *Convivio* (written in 1304). In the *Comedy*, we encounter the seven arts in the first section, the *Inferno*:

> We came to the foot of a noble castle,
> encircled seven times by towering walls,
> defended round about by a fair stream.
> Over this stream we moved as on dry land.
> Through seven gates I entered with these sages
> until we came to a fresh, green meadow.[27]

One scholar interprets this as follows:

> The fire that enveloped the castle of pagan learning was unique because within, though there had been separation from God, there had been no opposition. Entering the castle of seven walls by the gates of the seven liberal arts, Dante found himself among the representatives of the greatest thought of the past.[28]

In the *Convivio* or "Banquet," a later work, Dante associates the seven planetary heavens with the seven liberal arts:

> To the first seven [planetary spheres] correspond the seven sciences of the Trivium and the Quadrivium, namely Grammar, Dialectics, Rhetoric, Arithmetic, Music, Geometry, and Astrology. To the eighth sphere, namely the Starry Heaven, corresponds natural science, which is called Physics, and the first science, which is called Metaphysics; to the ninth sphere corresponds Moral Science; and to the still heaven corresponds Divine Science, which is called Theology.[29]

There are a few old Masonic legends beginning about 1350 regarding the seven arts that, in

William Preston's 1775 Lecture on the Liberal Arts

When they passed the columns, where did they arrive?
Having passed through the porch, at the entrance of which the two sacred columns were reared, the skilled craftsmen came to a winding staircase, that led to the middle chamber, where Solomon had ordered all the gifts of merit to be conferred. On every step of that staircase was stamped the name of a different art, and over each art was appointed a superintendent, to try the merit of the claimants in that art.

Who guarded the staircase?
At the bottom of the staircase was posted an ingenious craftsman to whom all who approached must submit their claims.

What was the duty of this craftsman?
The duty of this guard was not only to receive, examine, and arrange the claims, but to refer the candidates, who delivered them, to the superintendent, who was appointed to enquire into the abilities of each claimant. By this arrangement all attempts at imposition were prevented, and the merits of the industrious were duly honoured and rewarded.

Of how many steps is it said, did this staircase consist?
This staircase is said to have consisted of seven steps.

To what do those steps refer?
In reference to the seven liberal arts, one or other of which was considered as an essential qualification for preferment: every candidate was tried, and approved, in the art, in which he excelled, by the superintendent of that art; who was pledged to display his powers, and illustrate his excellence on the step, which was allotted to his profession.

How were these arts used?
These seven arts, which were marked as objects of merit, were thus named and arranged: Grammar, Rhetoric, Logic, Arithmetic, Geometry, Music, Astronomy, and in these arts the professors were appointed under Royal commission, to exemplify at stated periods their skill and talents.

   Grammar, the First step. On the first step, there the Grammarian usually displayed, the excellence of his art. He taught the proper arrangement of words, according to idiom or dialect; and how to speak or write a language, with justice and accuracy, according to reason and correct usage.

On the Second step, the Rhetorician displayed the powers of his art. He taught the mode of speaking copiously, and fluently, on any subject; not merely with propriety alone, but with all the advantages of force, and elegance; wisely contriving to captivate the hearer by the strength of argument, and beauty of expression.

On the Third step, the Logician exerted his talents, he taught the art of guiding reason discretionarily, in the general knowledge of things; and how we were to direct our enquiries at the truth: instructing his disciples to infer, deduce, and conclude, on a regular train of argument, according to certain premises laid down, or granted; and to employ their faculties of conceiving, reasoning, judging, and disposing in true gradation, till the point in question should be finally determined.

On the Fourth step, the Arithmetician distinguished his skill: he taught the powers and properties of numbers, by letters, tables, figures, and instruments, giving reasons and demonstrations, to find any certain number whose relation to another number was already known. To every mechanical branch or profession he recommended the virtues of his art.

On the Fifth step, the Geometrician displayed the superiority of his science: he treated on the powers, and properties of magnitude in general, where length, breadth, and thickness were considered. He taught the architect to construct his plans; the general to arrange his troops, the engineer to mark out ground for encampments the geographer to give us the dimensions of the world, delineate the extent of seas, and specify the divisions of Empires, kingdoms and provinces; and the astronomer to make his

observations, and fix the duration of times, and seasons. In short he proved Geometry to be the foundation of architecture, and the root of mathematics.

On the Sixth step, the Musician displayed his eminence, he taught the art of forming concords, and to compose delightful harmony by a proportion and arrangement of acute, grave, and mixed sounds. By a series of experiments he evinced the power of his art, with respect to tunes, and the intervals of sound only; and in his enquiry into the nature of the concords and discords he fixed the proportion between them by numbers.

On the Seventh step, the Astronomer vies to excel, he taught the art of reading the wonderful works of the Creator in the sacred pages, the celestial hemispheres; by observing the motion, measuring the distances, comprehending the magnitudes and calculating the periods, and eclipses of the heavenly bodies. The use of the globes, the system of the world, and the primary law of nature, were the subjects of his theme, and in the unparalleled instances of wisdom and goodness that were displayed through the whole of the creation, he traced the omnipotent Author by his works.

What were the effects that were derived from this establishment?
The effects of this establishment were at that time sensibly felt, under the sanction of the wisest Prince that ever reigned; the most eminent artificers were collected, instructed, and improved; talents and ingenuity were encouraged and protected; knowledge was spread and disseminated, and works of eminence were produced, which stand unrivalled, in the annals of history and fame.

my opinion, provide hints as to their more spiritual purpose. Older but similar legends occur in the surviving literature of the ancient Near East — even back to Babylonia.[30] The apocryphal *Life of Adam and Eve*, which survives in a Christian Latin version ultimately derived from a Hebrew original circa 100 BCE–200 CE, related that just before Eve's death, she called Seth and all of her other children and gave them a peculiar order:

> [...L]isten to me, my children! Make now tablets of stone and other tablets of clay and write in them all my life and your father's which you have heard and seen from us. If [God] should judge our race by water, the tablets of earth will dissolve and the tablets of stone will remain; but if he should judge our race by fire, the tablets of stone will break up and those of clay will be thoroughly baked.[31]

The book then relates that while many saw the tablets after the flood, only Solomon read them and understood them, as a result of which he established his Temple upon the site at which they were found.[32]

Other ancient accounts transform the tablets into pillars; the details of who creates the pillars and what knowledge is written upon them varies.[33] The oldest text that ties the seven liberal arts to the pillars is the *Chronicles of Jerahmeel*, a medieval text that compiled many ancient traditions. After noting that Zoroaster discovered "the art of Nagirā (נגירא)" or necromancy,[34] the account relates that he

> had written down the seven sciences (or arts) on fourteen pillars, seven of brass and seven of brick, so that they should be proof against the water — of the flood — and against the fire of the day of judgment.[35]

The early Masonic manuscripts known as the Old Charges generally retain the concept of the liberal arts inscribed upon the two antediluvian pillars, and sometimes claim that "both pillars were found, one by Pythagoras and one by Hermes, who each taught the secrets they found written thereon."[36]

Another early version of the story of the transmission of the arts and sciences comes from the Regius Poem (dated about 1390). Following the segment about the Quatuor Coronati ("Four Crowned Artisans") and the Tower of Babel — which was said to be built seven miles high — is the reference to the seven arts:

> Many years after the good scholar Euclyde
> Taught the craft of Geometry wonderfully wide.
> So he did at that time introduce
> Many other divers crafts
> Through the grace of Christ in Heaven.
> He established the Seven Sciences.[37]

In the Dowland MS. (c. 1550) we find basically the same story: It tells of how the worthy sciences were preserved through the Deluge. Simply, Lamech's children (one was Tubal-cain) knew God was going to destroy the world but did not know in what fashion — fire or water — so they chiseled their knowledge on two pillars of stone.[38]

Another tale is told in a seventeenth century copy of an earlier work called a *Commentary by Toz Graecus, philosopher of great renown, on the books given by Solomon to Rehoboam concerning the Secret of Secrets*. We are told that:

> The preface reveals that Solomon gathered his vast learning into a book intended for his son Rehoboam, which he locked up in an ivory coffer concealed in his tomb. Later Toz (Thoth) discovered it, and as he was weeping for his

Stained glass representation of St. Bernard of Clairvaux. Upper Rhine, circa 1450.

incapacity to understand its contents, an angel of the Lord came to reveal its meaning to him, but enjoined him not to disclose it to any but those who were worthy of it. We also learn, thanks to the *Liber de secretissimo philosophorum opere chemico* (fifteenth century) that Hermes traveled to the Valley of Hebron, where Adam was buried, and there found seven tablets of stone written before the Deluge, containing the doctrine of the seven liberal arts.[39]

In an article about the Royal Ark Mariner degree, the author R. M. Handfield-Jones, in speaking about the association of Noah with Freemasonry makes the following observation:

In the first known MS Constitution, the Regius Poem, there occurred on line 537 a passing reference to Noah and the Flood. From then onwards from the Cooke MS every Masonic Constitution contains allusions to Noah, not however to the Flood and the Ark but to his finding the two great pillars inscribed with the seven liberal arts and sciences. The date of the Regius poem is about 1390 but like the Cooke it bears evidence of being derived from an earlier document written in 1350. Here therefore as early as the middle of the 14th century we have the Noah story appearing in association with Masonry, but the flood and the Ark take a secondary place to the two pillars found by Noah *after* the Flood.[40]

In fact, representations of the seven liberal arts were emerging in many places during the Middle Ages. Some believe that the twelfth century stone carvings on Chartres Cathedral were the first personifications of the seven in the visual arts (they had, of course, been personified in literature since Martianus Capella's *De Nuptiis Philologiæ et Mercurii* in the fourth century). We find many examples in painting, such as a fourteenth-century fresco of Thomas Aquinas. It pictures Aquinas in the midst of a very crowded scene with figures representing saints, the virtues, the patriarchs, and at last the seven liberal arts. This fresco can be found on the walls of a Dominican convent in Florence, and there exist many similar artistic representations in manuscripts of the era.

In the first Book of Constitutions, published at the beginning of the era of organized Freemasonry in 1723, James Anderson wrote:

> Adam, our first parent, created after the Image of God, the great Architect of the Universe, must have had the Liberal Sciences, particularly Geometry, written on his Heart; for ever since the Fall, we find the Principles of it in the Heart of his Offspring.... [41]

William Preston's 1775 lecture on the liberal arts and sciences [see pages 43–44] went into eloquent detail regarding each of the seven disciplines.[42] These were directly adapted into the work taught by Thomas Smith Webb in North America in 1797, and retained by later editors such as Jeremy Ladd Cross in 1819 and Charles Whitlock Moore in 1843.[43] In England, the English Emulation ritual that developed after the 1813 union of the Antients and Moderns taught:

> Q: Why do seven or more make it [the Lodge] perfect?
> A: Because King Solomon was seven years and upwards in building, completing, and dedicating the Temple at Jerusalem to God's service.
> Q: They have a further allusion?
> A: To the seven liberal arts and sciences...[44]

The seven are then named individually and followed by a short definition of each, derived from Preston's earlier lectures.

Strange and Mixed Companies

This section introduces St. Bernard of Clairvaux, the Knights of the Temple, and Dante Alighieri. There are more than a few interesting interconnections between the three — some actual, some inferred. By bringing these to light here, I hope to demonstrate the high esteem in which the seven arts were once held.

ST. BERNARD OF CLAIRVAUX (1090–1153)

Bernard was born into a family of some nobility in the Burgundy region of France. His father was a knight, as were his brothers. By the time Bernard had reached his twenty-fifth birthday he had become the abbot of a Cistercian monastery. The Cistercians, by the way, were known for their architectural skill.

> Gothic appeared everywhere at the same time in the Christian west; always in the Benedictine or Cistercian abbeys, Cistercian above all.... Gothic appeared after the first Crusade and more particularly after the return in 1128 of the first nine Knights Templar.[45]

Another scholar puts it simply that "[t]he influence of Cistercian upon the first Gothic architecture is beyond question."[46] Bernard went on to become one of the most influential men in twelfth century Europe. By the time he died, he had written at least 3,500 pages of religious work. Although there are many colorful aspects of his life, there are only a few pertinent here, namely, his special type of mysticism, his connection with the Chartres Cathedral and his relation with the Knights Templar. Even after his death his influence was strong; we find him again portrayed in Dante's *Divine Comedy*.

Bernards' mystical theology was based on love and knowledge. He taught that there were four consecutive degrees in the soul's progress in experiencing God's love. The soul becomes more immersed in Divine Love as it conforms to Divine Will. The disorder of human life is ultimately due to the separation and conflict of the human will from the Divine Will. Changing and redeeming can only come about through love, in Bernard's view. It is only love that can unite the division of wills. That is why his mysticism has been labeled "affective mysticism" or "bride mysticism." The mystical union with God comes about through a union of wills, not personalities or beingness, and spirituality becomes almost a courtship between two lovers. One of his masterpieces is his eighty-six sermon mystical commentary on the esoteric symbolism of the Song of Songs attributed to King Solomon.[47] The mysticism of Bernard balanced contemplation and action. It was a process of bringing the will closer and closer to reflect the Divine Will through contemplation and bringing that Will into the world through action.

Another aspect of Bernard's theology was his dedication to the Holy Virgin. "He gave impetus to two devotions that flourished in the later Middle Ages, becoming major forces in subsequent spirituality: devotion to Mary and to the humanity of Christ."[48] Titus Burckhardt speaks of the ambiance of the times:

[...V]arious currents flowed together and formed a new and reawakened cult of the Holy Virgin: the longing for the Holy Land, the true home, the need to turn to the maternal mercy of God, and the chivalric cult of the celestial Lady as the epitome of nobility of soul, innocence

and beauty. St. Bernard himself, who knew how to call forth the highest spiritual powers of his contemporaries, is said to have been the first to use the chivalric mode of address Notre Dame (Our Lady) for the Mother of God.[49]

Bernard had many connections with both the cathedral and school at Chartres.

There were many points of contact between Bernard and the Knights Templar. The Council of Troyes (1128) set the regulations (the so-called Rule) by which the Templars would act. It was Bernard's cousin, Hugh of Payens, who became the first Grand Master of this Order that had been established in Jerusalem. And it was Hugh of Payens who requested Bernard to write his famous treatise *In Praise of the New Militia* (sometime between 1128–1136). Bernard was obviously torn in regards to the idea of monks (holy types) and knights (warrior types) and the problem of uniting them into one person. This was quite a struggle for Bernard but one he gradually resolved. Being that their duties lie in the Holy Land, Bernard wrote a collection of meditations for the Templars that were based upon the sacred sites of the area (such as the Temple, the cities of Bethlehem and Nazareth, on Calvary and the Holy Sepulcher) and events that occurred there. In this way, the knights could lead a contemplative life while "out in the field." Yet, the main point here is that the Cistercians were the guiding force of the Templars who later built castles and churches themselves.

Finally, it is well to remember St. Bernard's pivotal role in the *Divine Comedy*. The *Commedia* is a story about Dante's journey through the three regions of hell, purgatory, and paradise. On this journey he describes what he experiences and who he meets at every level, and sometimes sublevels of these three zones. He has three guides through this process. Initially, he is led through the underworld realms by the Roman poet Virgil. Then he is guided by his beloved Beatrice, an embodiment of all that is good and beautiful, who she leads him to higher and higher realms — almost but just short of the highest sphere of Paradise. It is at this point that he meets St. Bernard of Clairvaux, who then guides his vision to the ultimate sphere.

THE KNIGHTS TEMPLAR
AND THEIR LEGACY

The Knights of the Temple were started by a few knights probably in 1119 about eighteen years after the first crusade. Their first Grand Master was Hugh of Payens. By 1128 they were officially established by the Council of Troyes, but consisted of only nine knights. They gradually grew in power and prestige to become a major power in Europe. Malcolm Barber, the leading scholarly historian of the subject, describes the pinnacle of their success:

> During the thirteenth century the Order may have had as many as 7,000 knights, sergeants and serving brothers, and priests, while its associate members, pensioners, officials, and subjects numbered many times that figure. By about 1300 it had built a network of at least 870 castles, preceptories, and subsidiary houses, examples of which could be found in almost every country in Western Christendom.[50]

This all ended with the mass arrests of the knights in France in October on Friday the thirteenth, 1307. The twenty-second and last Grand Master Jacques de Molay, after being held and tortured for almost seven years, was executed March 18, 1314. But not all of the Templars could be arrested. Despite the popular legend of their complete eradication, the fact is that some of those who were arrested were later released for various reasons. Again Barber explains that even after being arrested and later released: "Most of those…received pensions and some even continued to live in former Templar houses; others were sent to the houses of other orders like those of the Cistercians and Augustinians, especially in England…."[51] And then some just went back into society. Professor Antoine Faivre of the Sorbonne tells us that "the Knights Templar supported and considerably developed the freecrafts and, after the disappearance of the order, entered into the corporations of builders."[52] Things were easier in Portugal for the Templars. In 1319, the Militia of Christ was formed and some former Templars were members. But at this time the religious military orders were going out of public favor and secular knighthood became increasingly popular. Some of the more interesting orders to Freemasons (because they are mentioned in our lecture on the apron) included the Order of the Garter (England, 1348), the Order of the Star (France, 1351), and the Order of the Golden Fleece (Belgium, 1429). Faivre notes the enduring influence of this last society upon later philosophical developments:

> The year 1429 was marked by an event having a major influence on the esoteric thought of modern times; this was the creation of the Order of the Golden Fleece by Philippe the Good, duke of Burgundy. … The Order possessed a beautiful symbolism in dress and ritual, over which generations of alchemists would ponder, at least up to the eighteenth century.[53]

The Orders of chivalry were springing up all over Europe, often with the central theme of the idealized woman, who—much like

Dante's—appears as the guide for man on his quest. The concept was also expressed by the troubadours, the lyric poets of the eleventh through the thirteenth centuries in France who sung of chivalry and courtly love.

DANTE ALIGHIERI
AND HIS MASTERFUL VISION

Dante began work on the *Commedia* in 1302, and started the *Convivio* in 1304. These works offer a striking cosmological map of the three zones of the universe as understood in the Western tradition. Titus Burckhardt points out that:

> The type of epic poem describing the path of the knower of God in symbolical form, is not rare in the Islamic world. It may be surmised that certain of these works were translated into the Provençal language, and we know that the community of the 'Fedeli d'Amore' to which Dante belonged, was in communication with the Order of the Temple, which was established in the East and open to the intellectual world of Islam.[54]

The philosopher René Guénon, who wrote a book specifically on the esoteric symbolism in Dante's work, comments upon some artifacts bearing upon this last point:

> In the Vienna Museum there are two medallions, one representing Dante....[O]n the reverse side both bear the letters F.S.K.I.P.F.T., which Aroux interprets as: *Frater Sacroe Kadosch, Imperialis Principatus, Frater Templarius.* [...W]e think it should read *Fidei Sanctoe Kadosch.* The Association of the *Fede Santa*, of which Dante seems to have been a leader, was a tertiary order of Templar filiation, justifying the name *Frater Templarius*; its dignitaries bore the title of *Kadosch*,

a Hebrew word meaning 'holy' or 'consecrated', which has been preserved to our days in the high grades of Masonry. It is not without reason then that Dante takes St. Bernard, who established the rule of the Order of the Temple, as his guide for the completion of his own celestial journey.[55]

In trying to understand Dante's work, Guénon considers the significance of the symbolic regions that Dante illustrates in the *Divine Comedy*. The hints Guénon says are in the later work, the *Convivio* or Banquet where Dante associates the seven liberal arts with the celestial realms. Dante says: "To see what is meant by this third heaven…I say that by heaven I mean 'science,' and by heavens, 'the sciences.'"[56] Guénon says that: "These regions are in reality so many different states, and the heavens are, literally, 'spiritual hierarchies', that is to say, degrees of initiation."[57] And he links them all:

> But what exactly are these 'sciences' understood under the symbolic designation of the 'heavens', and must we see therein an allusion to the 'seven liberal arts' so often mentioned elsewhere by Dante and his contemporaries? What leads us to think that this must be the case is that according to Aroux, 'the Cathars had, as early as the twelfth century, some signs of recognition, passwords, and astrological doctrine (they conducted their initiations at the vernal equinox). Their scientific system was founded on the doctrine of correspondences: Grammar corresponded to the Moon, Dialectic to Mercury, Rhetoric to Venus, Music to Mars, Geometry to Jupiter, Astronomy to Saturn, and Arithmetic or Illumined Reason to the Sun.' Accordingly, to the seven planetary spheres—the first seven of Dante's nine heavens—corresponded the seven liberal arts respectively; and precisely

these same designations are depicted on the seven rungs of the left upright of the *Ladder of the Kadosch* (30th degree of Scottish Masonry).[58]

We can conclude this section by pointing out the incredible tapestry interwoven in this period. We know of the connections between Bernard and the Cistercians with the Cathedral and School of Chartres (just to name one actually), and the Templars. We know their architectural influence upon both. We also know the importance the seven liberal arts were to architecture and theology. And we know that they were taught extensively at the school of Chartres; so much so, it is generally accepted that the seven liberal arts reached their zenith at this place. Later we see Dante represent them in a celestial and spiritual way. We also see a version of the Celestial Lady in Dante that we saw earlier with Bernard and as well in the stonework of Chartres where personifications of the seven arts surround the Virgin. It is natural that this leads us to a closer examination of the deeper meanings that may be associated with the seven liberal arts, and how these arts inform the spiritual dimension of architecture.

The Vision of the Temple

MYSTICAL ARCHITECTURE

One way of understanding our work as Freemasons is the idea that we are building "that house not made with hands, eternal in the heavens." We have our symbolic tools to build and design, our arts and sciences to inform and guide our work, and the prototype to emulate — King Solomon's Temple.

Throughout history there have been many monuments that have sought to embody that very spirit in order to be a living icon for the world to see. The Cathedral of Chartres is considered by many to be one of the finest examples. Like many Gothic cathedrals, it was dedicated to the Holy Mother, herself a common symbol of the human soul. Titus Burckhardt explains:

According to the Medieval theologians the Virgin Mary, by virtue of the innate perfection of her soul, possessed all the wisdom of which man is capable. A direct reference to this wisdom is to be found in the allegories of the seven liberal arts which, just outside an inner circle of adoring angels, decorate the *tympanum* of the Door of the Virgin. In the Medieval context the seven sciences were not exclusively empirical sciences, as are those we know today. They were the expression of so many faculties of the soul, faculties demanding harmonious development. This is why they were also called arts…. The seven planets, on the other hand, govern, according to the ancient viewpoint, the world of the soul. And Mary is the human soul in all its perfection.[59]

We can naturally come to the question of how do we express and develop these faculties and where does it lead us? Burckhardt answers that there is a "reciprocal relationship between knowledge and will," and that "Knowledge of the eternal truths is potentially present in the human spirit or intellect, but its unfolding is directly conditioned by the will…"[60] This very Platonic sentiment is echoed in the Masonic teaching that "a fund of science and industry is implanted in man."[61] So if we assume that knowledge of the eternal truths is available and within the human soul, the question then becomes how do we gain access into that interior Temple? Burckhardt has already answered by saying that the key is the *will*. To fully understand the solution it is necessary to understand the mindset of the people who inhabited the medieval world. In their world-view, everyday life was lived in the presence of the supernatural, and under the notion that one could behold at least part of sacred reality with the senses. Therefore, to approach the Cathedral was to be on the threshold of the spiritual dimension, for it was considered to actually be a representation of ultimate reality.

The seven arts guided the intellect to approach the hidden light behind the world. The invisible, underlying structure of Reality — the Truth — could be apprehended, and this apprehension had the senses as its foundation. So the temple of God demanded exact building codes — and the prototype for the House of God was Solomon's Temple. The key to building the Temple was geometry. One author on the subject of sacred geometry explains that:

> In the same way that the Logos is a mediator between unity and multiplicity, the temple is a mediator between heaven and earth, the timeless and the temporal. Therefore, ever since the earliest times, religious architecture has been rooted in the timeless principles of "sacred geometry." By basing sacred architecture on the principles of transcendent form and harmony, temple architects expressed the harmony of heaven on earth. Not only do ancient temples express this harmony, but, through the use of gematria, they were designed to attract the spirit to which they were consecrated.[62]

Included in the concept of sacred geometry are all the liberal arts. If nature is the true temple of God's dwelling, then cosmic and natural laws must be the trestle board. These laws are the laws discovered by the practice of the seven arts. These include such things as the intercon-nection between numbers, ratios and proportions in such areas as arithmetic, geometry, music and astronomy. It was thought that the same laws linked and even bound the microcosm to the macrocosm.

The masters of Chartres (and Dante after them) were inheritors of the tradition of Augustine, the Platonists and the Pythagoreans. Like these philosophers of old they considered geometry to have an anagogic function: "that is, its ability to lead the mind from the world of appearances to the contemplation of the divine order."[63] Or, in other words, "that number may guide the intellect from the perception of created things to the invisible truth in God."[64] It might be said that it was the combination of the Platonic cosmology and the spirituality of Clairvaux that produced Gothic art.

Another very pertinent concept we find at Chartres is that God is the architect of the universe. The teachers of the school of Chartres:

> identify the Platonic world soul with the Holy Ghost in its creative and ordering effect upon matter; and they conceive this effect as musical consonance. The harmony it establishes throughout the cosmos is represented, however, not only as a musical composition but also as an artistic one, more specifically, as a work of architecture. [...F]or the theologians of Chartres, the notion of the cosmos as a work of architecture and of God as it architect has a special significance, since they assume a twofold act of creation: the creation of chaotic matter and the creation of cosmos out of chaos. Since the Greek word kosmos signified ornament as well as order, it was plausible to view matter as the building material, the creation proper as the 'adorning' of matter by the artful imposition of an architectural order. In the Platonic cosmology, moreover, the masters of Chartres

could detect the design and method according to which the divine architect had built the universe, the cosmic temple.... [65]

This dominant view is also thought to have caused a sociological phenomenon. Here is another fact that should be of particular interest to Freemasons in search of their roots. It is interesting to realize that clerics were mostly responsible for building, and the term *architectis* was not used very often. But:

the revival of the term in the mid-thirteenth century coincided exactly with the sociological change that transformed the humble master mason into the architect of the thirteenth century, no longer considered a mere craftsman but the 'scientist' or *theoreticus* of his art.[66]

It was then considered that only he who had mastered the seven liberal arts was entitled to the title of "architect."[67]

[...I]t was the School of Chartres that dramatized the image of the architect...by depicting God as a master builder, a *theoreticus* creating without toil or effort by means of an architectural science that is essentially mathematical. The Platonists of Chartres, moreover, also defined the laws according to which the cosmic edifice had been composed.... And in submitting to geometry the medieval architect felt that he was imitating the work of his divine master.[68]

We could, as well, characterize it as participating in the divine work.

Another aspect of the Gothic cathedral was its impressive advancement in the use of light. Gothic architecture provided opportunities for more light:

In the Cathedral of Chartres the architect has realized the cosmological order of luminosity and proportion to the exclusion of all other architectural motifs and with a perfection never achieved before. Light transfigures and orders the composition in the stained-glass windows. Numbers, the number of perfect proportion, harmonize all elements of the building. Light and harmony...are not merely images of heaven, symbolic or aesthetic attributes. Medieval metaphysics conceived them as the formative and ordering principles of creation, principles, however, that only in the heavenly spheres are present with unadulterated clarity. Light and harmony have precisely this ordering function in the Gothic cathedral.[69]

The Art of Memory

The practice of the art of memory developed to a very high level in the Medieval world. This practice was done by memorizing a series of places such as that found in a building. Within these rooms, one mentally establishes other images to serve as reminders of whatever is intended to be remembered or meditated upon. Mary Carruthers relates in her work, *The Book of Memory*, that records indicate that the art of memory was cultivated at Chartres.[70] Its spiritual employment is illustrated by the reference to the word *arca*, which means a wooden chest or box used for storage.

But there is another meaning of *arca* which is associated from earliest times with the process of Scriptural *lectio* and study. As *arca sapientiæ*, one's memory is the ideal product of a medieval education, laid out in organized *loci*. One designs and builds one's own memory according to one's talent, opportunities, and energy. That makes it a construction, an *ædificatio*. As some-

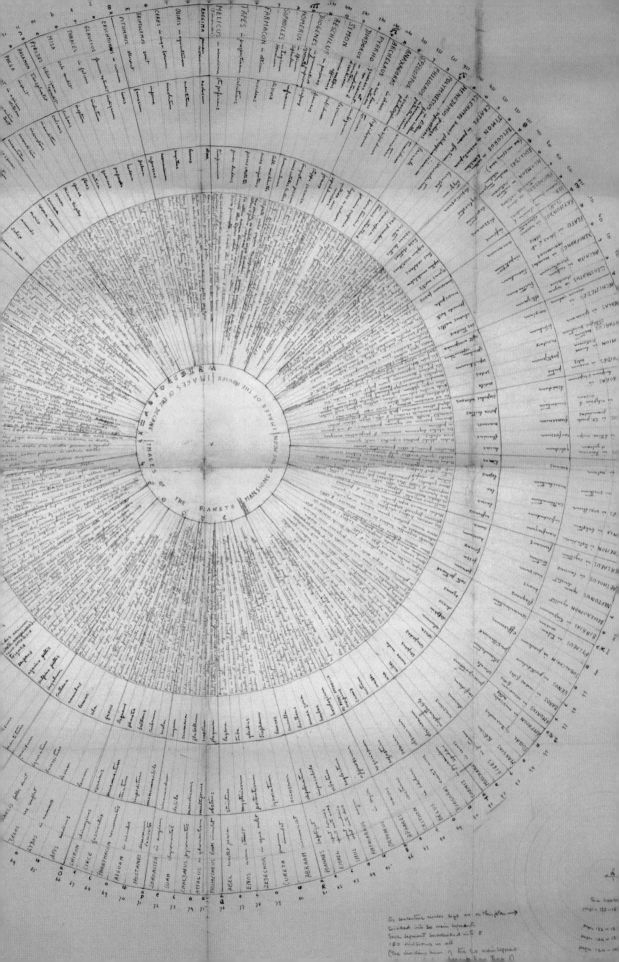

thing to be built, the trained memory is an *arca* in the sense understood by the Biblical object called Noah's Ark, the construction of which occupies some detail in Genesis, and the Ark of the Covenant, into which the books of the Law were placed.... [71]

The reason one might wish to practice the art of memory, apart from the ability to retain an extraordinary amount of "book knowledge," is explained by the Persian philosopher Avicenna (980–1037 CE). He taught that there is a connection between memory and spiritual experience. As Carruthers summarizes:

> The images produced during dreams and trances will disappear unless they are associated with images that are already in memory storage, already familiar and accessible to recollection. Thus even direct inspiration requires the immediate assistance of human memory, though in a way more mysterious than that of ordinary dreaming or consciously controlled recollection.[72]

In Augustine's *Confessions* we read that he finds God through the memory.[73] Augustine's teaching is a direct adaptation of the Platonic concept that knowledge of the divine is a type of recollection or remembrance. The ancient Greeks called it *anamnēsis*. According to this perspective, knowledge about the ultimate nature of things is buried deep in our minds, "lost" only to the extent that it is generally forgotten. This knowledge is regained piecemeal through the random lessons and experiences of life, or better yet more systematically through the pursuit of philosophical education. Gregory Shaw describes it as

◀ Frances Yates' reconstruction of Giordano Bruno's memory wheel, as described in his book, *De Umbris Idearum*, published in 1582.

a process of reawakening by means of contacts with the sensible world that functioned as mnemonic prods, reminding the soul of the Platonic Forms. Theurgy should be seen as the development and translation of this epistemological theory into a ritual praxis where the prods of sensate experience were carefully controlled in rites designed to awaken the soul to the Forms.[74]

In this way, it was believed, externally performed ritual (properly designed and executed) is able to help us as we search the inner reaches of our souls for the "deep memory" or recollection of eternal truth.

There were many systems of training the memory. The development of these systems gradually became extremely elaborate. One example of this complexity is found in the treatise on memory by Johannes Romberch (1480–1532). Frances Yates explains Romberch's system as using the "cosmos as a place system," encompassing

> the spheres of the elements, of the planets, of the fixed stars, and above them the celestial spheres and those of the nine orders of angels.... This type of artificial memory may be called the Dantesque type...because Dante was influenced by such an interpretation of artificial memory....[75]

Giulio Camillo (1480–1544), who was one of the most famous men of the sixteenth century, constructed an elaborate wooden memory theater. Yates gives an account of its complexity:

> The theater rises in seven grades or steps, which are divided by seven gangways representing the seven planets. [...T]he solitary spectator stands where the stage would be and looks to-

wards the auditorium gazing at the images on the seven times seven gates on the seven rising grades. [...T]he whole system of the Theatre rests basically upon seven pillars, the seven pillars of Solomon's House of Wisdom. ... By these columns, signifying most stable eternity, we are to understand the seven Sephiroth of the supercelestial world, which are the seven measures of the fabric of the celestial and inferior worlds, in which are contained the Ideas of all things both in the celestial and in the inferior worlds. ... As Sephiroth in the supercelestial world they are here equated with the Platonic ideas. Camillo is basing his memory system on first causes, on the Sephiroth, on the Ideas; these are to be the 'eternal places' of his memory.[76]

And his way of using it is illustrated by the following description:

Thus, following the custom in ancient theatres in which the most important people sat in the lowest seats, Camillo has placed in his lowest grade the seven essential measures on which, according to magico-mystical theory, all things here below depend, the seven planets. Once these have been organically grasped, imprinted on memory with their images and characters, the mind can move from this middle celestial world in either direction; up into the supercelestial world of the Ideas, the Sephiroth and the angels, entering Solomon's Temple of Wisdom.... [77]

The result of this practice is nothing short of profound:

In this atmosphere, the relationship between man, the microcosm, and the world, the macrocosm, takes on a new significance. The microcosm can fully understand and fully re-member the macrocosm, can hold it within his divine *mens* or memory. ... That there is a strong Cabalist influence on the Theatre is obvious. ... For Camillo, it is the correspondence of the seven planetary measures of the celestial world with the supercelestial Sephiroth which gives the Theatre its prolongation up into the supercelestial world, into the abyss of the divine wisdom and the mysteries of the Temple of Solomon.[78]

In much of this work, the essential idea is to reproduce the celestial world within. Giordano Bruno's (1548–1600) work continues the same theme:

In relation to the fundamental zodiacal images, the planet images, moon station images, houses of the horoscope images of Bruno's list of magic images, move on the wheels of memory, forming and reforming the patterns of the universe from a celestial level. And the power to do this depends on the Hermetic philosophy, that man is in his origin divine, and organically related to the star-governors of the world. In 'your primordial nature' the archetypal images exist in a confused chaos; the magic memory draws them out of chaos and restores their order, gives back to man his divine powers.[79]

The development of the art of memory grew to encompass a mental representation of the entire cosmos as conceived in medieval times. Its use became as an object of contemplation through the use of will and imagination. Much of the structure of the process was inspired by the Hermetic sciences including kabbalah and astrology as well as Pythagorean number mysticism. As the building of this cosmic temple proceeded, it provided the necessary link of the mind with the divine world. Our journey has taught us that it is the understanding of the Pythagorean and Platonic view of the universe as well as the knowledge of the Hermetic art that provides us with the key to uniting the microcosm with the macrocosm, heaven and earth, and rediscovering that which was lost.

Conclusion

We now find that we have come full circle and have ended up back to the two pillars — the opening subject. From these old tales we remember that one pillar was found by Hermes and the other was found by Pythagoras. Remember also that within these two pillars the whole wisdom of the world was said to be inscribed. And this wisdom was divided into basically seven categories — the seven liberal arts. From these old tales we can receive some glimmer of the high esteem in which these arts and sciences were held. They were not only tales told among the public but were woven into the old Masonic legends.

We then considered the role of the Cistercians on Gothic architecture and the building crafts and that one special monk, St. Bernard, having influence all over Europe, promoted the devotion to the Blessed Virgin, developed a mysticism based on love and set down the Rule for the Knights Templar. The Templars increased in power and influence, built castles and churches all over Europe, had numerous contacts with the religious orders in the Holy Land, and after their suppression, many went into the building trades or back to the monastaries. We know that the School of Chartres studied deeply the Platonic, Neoplatonic, and Pythagorean philosophy and blended it with Christianity. The seven liberal arts were developed to their zenith at this time and place — scholars from every part of Europe went to study there. We

examined how the Cathedral was a symbol of the Holy Virgin (that also represents the human soul in its perfection), and it was the study of the seven liberal arts that promoted this accomplishment. We then considered Dante's alleged involvement with the Fideli d'Amore and his masterpiece of the *Commedia* which represents the Idealized Woman and St. Bernard as his guides to the highest spiritual realms.

In the final section, the subject shifted to the human endeavor of building with the express purpose of representing the spiritual dimension. Understanding the nature of the spiritual dimension demanded extensive study of the seven liberal arts so that what was built was in harmony with and embodied the divine. We also discussed how at one point there developed the idea that only one who had mastered the seven arts could be designated an architect. From there this paper considered the development of the art of memory utilizing temple design to enhance its purpose. And, that some practitioners incorporated kabbalistic, hermetic, astrological and numerological symbolism to develop this art into a spiritual practice. It was considered that developing mental representations to mirror the eternal and unchanging divine world and processes would bring about spiritual revelations. In other words, the practices would aid the soul in its ascent to the divine world. It would, surely, give one the vision of the celestial temple.

A number of eminent scholars — including Frances Yates, David Stevenson, and Marsha Keith Schuchard — have theorized that the origins of the fraternity of Freemasonry can be found emerging from this background.[80]

Stevenson notes that the Second Schaw Statutes of 1599 command the leaders of lodges to "tak tryall of the art of memorie and science thairof, of euerie fallowe of craft and euerie prenteiss,"[81] and this, with other evidence, led him to conclude that:

> [...]t is not implausible to think of William Schaw as seeing one aspect of the secret lodges he created as being a grafting of the ambitions that led to the founding of secret Hermetic societies onto a craft which already claimed that it had a connection with Hermes.... In this light, the core of ritual which lay at the heart of the new lodges can be seen as involving them in some sense in the Hermetic quest. ... One branch of the Hermetic quest centred attention on the art of memory...a technique which could harness mystical or magical powers in the pursuit of the lost wisdom of the ancients and of revelation of the divine.[82]

While it has been popular to regard the modern fraternity as merely a romantic continuation of the building guilds, it is generally overlooked that this does not necessarily translate into the humble and nonphilosophical origin so often imagined. The operative stonemasons — especially the masters and architects among them — were often pursuing lofty spiritual ambitions.

The central importance of the liberal arts and sciences in both operative and speculative Freemasonry may represent an important key to understanding our past, and brightening our future. Some are concerned that the fraternity appears to be diminishing in recent decades. But the tradition that Freemasonry perpetuates and is the foremost custodian of remains vibrant, and it is my conviction that this erosion is not inevitable if the fraternity will renew itself by a fresh look at its original purposes.

The key to this refreshment is a revival of the means by which a speculative Mason becomes an architect of the soul. And the means, my brothers, are the study and practice of the seven liberal arts. ✦

Notes

The first part of this paper was originally prepared by W∴ Bro∴ Worrel for the Northern California Research Lodge in March, 1997. It was later presented at a semiannual meeting of the Philalethes Society, in San Diego on September 27, 1997. The author made major revisions to the manuscript in January 2002 and August 2008. The second section of the paper was written in 2008–2009 for *Ahiman*, which is pleased to finally present the revised edition in its totality. A highly abridged version will be found in the Spring 2010 edition of *Philalethes*.

1. Harry L. Haywood, *Symbolical Masonry: An Interpretation of the Three Degrees* (Washington, D.C.: Masonic Service Association, 1923), 216.

2. Ibid., 237. Haywood is here arguing that the liberal arts are useful enough to be "retained," because Roscoe Pound, a prominent Freemason of the day who became Dean of the Harvard Law School, had published *Lectures on the Philosophy of Freemasonry* (Anamosa, Iowa: National Masonic Research Society, 1915), in which he argued strongly that the Prestonian lectures regarding the arts and sciences should be scrapped as outdated. They should be replaced, he said, with new ones "which set forth a regular system of modern knowledge demonstrated on the clearest principles and established in the firmest foundation." (19) Pound particularly stressed the notion that then-current theories of "so-

cial science" should be taught in the Lodges. (Ibid.) Thankfully, this disastrous call for revision was never embraced.

3. Henry Pelham Holmes Bromwell, *Restorations of Masonic Geometry and Symbolry* (Denver, Col.: The H. P. H. Bromwell Masonic Publishing Company, 1905), 355.

4. Robert Hewitt Brown, *Stellar Theology and Masonic Astronomy* (New York: D. Appleton, 1882), 57.

5. W. Kirk MacNulty, *Freemasonry: A Journey through Ritual and Symbol* (New York: Thames & Hudson, 1991), 23.

6. George H. Steinmetz, *Freemasonry: Its Hidden Meaning* (New York: Macoy, 1948), 120.

7. Ibid., 124.

8. Albert Pike (uncredited), *Legenda* XIX *to* XXX (Charleston, S.C.: Supreme Council, n.d.), 134–35. Modern students of the Scottish Rite may locate this essay in Arturo de Hoyos, *The Scottish Rite Ritual Monitor and Guide*, Second Edition (Washington, DC: Supreme Council, 2009), beginning at p. 719.

9. W. L. Wilmshurst, *The Ceremony of Passing* (London: J. M. Watkins), 20.

10. Ibid., 21.

11. Paul Abelson, *The Seven Liberal Arts: A Study in Mediæval Culture* (New York: Russell & Russell, 1965), 9.

12. William Harris Stahl & Richard Johnson, *Martianus Capella and the Seven Liberal Arts* (New York: Columbia University Press, 1971), 1:91.

13. René M. Querido, *The Golden Age of Chartres* (New York: Anthroposophic Press, 1987), 21.

14. Raymond Klibansky, "The School of Chartres," in M. Clagett, G. Post & R. Reynolds (Eds.), *Twelfth-Century Europe and the Foundations of Modern Society* (Madison, Wis.: University of Wisconsin Press, 1961), 13.

15. Adolf Katzenellenbogen, "The Representation of the seven liberal arts," in M. Clagett, G. Post & R. Reynolds (Eds.), *Twelfth-Century Europe and the Foundations of Modern Society* (Madison, Wis.: University of Wisconsin Press, 1961), 39.

16. Klibansky, "The School of Chartres,"

17. Ibid.

18. David E. Luscombe in Paul Edwards (Ed.), *The Encyclopedia of Philosophy* (New York: Macmillan, 1967), 1:83.

19. Edward F. Edinger, *Anatomy of the Psyche: Alchemical Symbolism in Psychotherapy* (La Salle, Ill.: Open Court, 1985), 117–18.

20. Ibid., 123.

21. The *or ha-ganuz* is a term used widely in medieval Jewish mystical texts to refer to the original light of Genesis, which was understood to be of a higher form than mere physical light, and which is hidden away except for the elect.

22. E. A. Wallis Budge, *Egyptian Magic* (London: Tuebner, 1899), 52–53.

23. Mircea Eliade, *Shamanism: Archaic Techniques of Ecstasy* (New York: Pantheon, 1964), 259.

24. Ibid., 488–89.

25. Plato, *Republic* 522a–528e.

26. Stahl & Johnson, *Martianus Capella*, 1:24.

27. *Inferno* IV, 106–111 (trans. by Robert Hollander and Jean Hollander).

28. See Helen Flanders Dunbar, *Symbolism in Medieval Thought and Its Consummation in the Divine Comedy* (New York: Russell & Russell, 1961), 172.

29. Dante, *Convivio* II, 13.8 (trans. by Richard H. Lansing).

30. Douglas Knoop & G. P. Jones, *The Genesis of Freemasonry* (Manchester, UK: Manchester University Press, 1949), 67.

31. *The Life of Adam and Eve* 50.1–2 (trans. by M. D. Johnson). Latin: Sed audite me, filii mei! facite ergo tabulas lapideas et alias tabulas luttea et scribite in his omnem vitam meam et patris vestri quae a nobis audistis et vidistis. Si per aquam iudicabit genus nostrum, tabulae de terra solventur et tabulae lapideae perma nebunt. si autem per ignem iudicabit genus nostrum, tabulae lapideae solventur et de terra luteae decoquentur.

32. *The Life of Adam and Eve* 51.3–8. Latin: Et post diluvium a multis videbantur hominibus tabulae illae scriptæ et a nemine legebantur. Salomon autem sapiens vidit scripturam et deprecatus est dominum et apparuit ei angelus domini dicens: ego sum qui tenui manum Seth, ut scriberet cum digito suo lapides istos, et eris sciens scripturam, ut cognoscas et in-

telligas quid contineant lapides isti omnes et ubi fuerit oratorium, ubi Adam et Eva adorabant dominum deum. et oportet te ibi aedificare templum domini id est domum orationis. Tunc Salomon supplevit templum domini dei et vocavit literas illas achiliacas hoc est sine verborum doctrina scriptas digito Seth, tenens manum eius angelus domini.

33. Knoop & Jones, *Genesis of Freemasonry*, 68.

34. Chronicles of Jerahmeel 32.4 (trans. Moses Gaster).

35. Ibid.

36. Knoop & Jones, *Genesis of Freemasonry*, 69.

37. Halliwell MS., lines 551–56.

38. William James Hughan, *The Old Charges of British Freemasons* (London: Simpkin, Marshall & Co., 1872), 25–26.

39. Antoine Faivre, *The Eternal Hermes: From Greek God to Alchemical Magus* (Grand Rapids, Mich.: Phanes Press, 1995), 95.

40. R. M. Handfield-Jones, *The Royal Ark Mariner Degree: Its Origin and History* (London: Grand Mark Lodge, 1974), 15-16.

41. James Anderson, *The Constitutions of the Free-Masons* (London: W. Hunter, J. Senex & J. Hooke, 1723), 1.

42. Colin Dyer, *William Preston and His Work* (Shepperton, UK: Lewis Masonic, 1987), 250–51.

43. Thomas Smith Webb, *The Freemason's Monitor, or Illustrations of Masonry in Two Parts* (Albany: Spencer & Webb, 1797), 79–82; Jeremy Ladd Cross, *The True Masonic Chart, or Hieroglyphic Monitor*, 4th ed. (New Haven, CT: J. L. Cross, 1826), 30–32; Charles Whitlock Moore & S. W.B. Carnegy, *The Trestleboard* (Boston: Charles W. Moore, 1843), 35–37.

44. *The Complete Workings of Craft Freemasonry*, rev. ed. (Hersham, UK: Lewis Masonic, 1982), 256. The earliest appearance of this particular wording may be in Richard Carlile's exposure of the Craft, printed in his periodical, *The Republican* 12(1825): 77.

45. Louis Charpentier, *The Mysteries of Chartres Cathedral* (New York: Avon, 1980), 36.

46. Otto von Simson, *The Gothic Cathedral*, 3d edition (Princeton, NJ: Princeton University Press, 1988), 56.

47. Translated in a four volume set: Bernard of Clairvaux, *On the Song of Songs*, trans. Irene Edmonds (Kalamazoo, Mich.: Cisterian Publications, 1980).

48. Ewert H. Cousins, preface to *Bernard of Clairvaux: Selected Works*, ed. Gillian R. Evans (St. Paul, Minn.: Paulist Press, 1987), 5.

49. Titus Burckhardt, *Chartres and the Birth of the Cathedral* (Bloomington, Ind.: World Wisdom, 1996), 60.

50. Malcolm Barber, *The New Knighthood: A History of the Order of the Temple* (Cambridge, UK: Cambridge University Press, 1995), 1.

51. Ibid., 304.

52. Antoine Faivre, "Ancient and Medieval Sources of Modern Esoteric Movements," in *Modern Esoteric Spirituality*, ed. Antoine Faivre & Jacob Needleman (New York: Crossroad, 1992), 51.

53. Faivre, "Ancient and Medieval Sources," 69.

54. Titus Burckhardt, *The Mirror of the Intellect* (Albany, N.Y.: State University of New York Press, 1987), 96.

55. René Guénon, *The Esoterism of Dante* (Hillsdale, N.Y.: Sophia Perennis, 2004), 5.

56. Dante, *Convivio* II, 13.1–2 (trans. by Richard H. Lansing).

57. Guénon, *Esoterism of Dante*, 6.

58. Ibid., 6–7.

59. Burckhardt, *Mirror of the Intellect*, 77.

60. Ibid., 89.

61. This statement is commonly found in American Masonic ritual, and originated in William Preston's May 21, 1772 address to the Grand Officers: "Operative masonry furnishes us with dwellings, and convenient shelters from the vicissitudes and the inclemencies of the seasons. It displays human wisdom in a proper arrangement of materials, and demonstrates that a fund of science and industry is implanted in the rational species for the most wise, salutary, and beneficent purposes." William Preston, *Illustrations of Masonry*, 1st ed. (London: J. Williams, 1772), 13. This notion of innate knowledge is expressed in the opening sentences of Anderson's *Constitutions* of 1723: "Adam, our first parent, created after the Image of God, the great Architect of the Universe,

must have had the Liberal Sciences, particularly Geometry, written on his Heart; for ever since the Fall, we find the Principles of it in the Heart of his Offspring...." Anderson, *Constitutions*, 1. The teaching itself is one of the core Masonic principles, implicit in the Old Charges that pre-date the Grand Lodge era.

62. David R. Fideler, *Jesus Christ: Sun of God* (Wheaton, Ill.: Quest, 1993), 216.

63. Simson, *Gothic Cathedral*, 22.

64. Ibid., 25.

65. Ibid., 29.

66. Ibid., 30.

67. Ibid., 31.

68. Ibid., 31, 35.

69. Ibid., 228.

70. Mary Carruthers, *The Book of Memory: A Study of Memory in Medieval Culture* (Cambridge, UK: Cambridge University Press, 2008), 111.

71. Ibid., 51.

72. Ibid., 75.

73. Augustine of Hippo, *Confessions* 10.25–26.

74. Gregory Shaw, *Theurgy and the Soul: The Neoplatonism of Iamblichus* (Philadelphia: Pennsylvania State University Press, 1971), 24.

75. Frances A. Yates, *The Art of Memory* (Chicago: University of Chicago Press, 1966), 115–16.

76. Ibid., 136–37.

77. Ibid., 138–39.

78. Ibid., 148.

79. Ibid., 217.

80. See Yates, *Art of Memory*, 303–05, for the initial suggestion. Later researchers detail potentially supportive evidence in David Stevenson, *The Origins of Freemasonry: Scotland's Century, 1590–1710* (Cambridge, UK: Cambridge University Press, 1988); David Stevenson, *The First Freemasons*, 2d ed. (Edinburgh: Grand Lodge of Scotland, 2001); and Marsha Keith Schuchard, *Restoring the Temple of Vision: Cabalistic Freemasonry and Stuart Culture* (Leiden: Brill, 2002).

81. Stevenson, *Origins of Freemasonry*, 45.

82. Stevenson, *The First Freemasons*, 6.

The Memory Lodge: Masonic Applications of the Art of Memory

Erik L. Arneson

The attentive ear receives the sound from the instructive tongue, and [our] sacred mysteries are safely lodged in the repository of faithful breasts. The tools and implements of architecture—symbols the most expressive!—imprint on the memory wise and serious truths, and transmit unimpaired, through the succession of ages, the excellent tenets of this institution.

William Preston
Illustrations of Masonry, 1772

Sensation and memory, then,
are not passivity but power.

Plotinus, *The Enneads* 4.6.3

IN THE AGES before printing, a good memory was a prized possession, and people honed theirs using ancient techniques originally developed in the classical world. There is little doubt today that the *ars memoria*, or art of memory, played an important part in the development of Renaissance magic and philosophy. Though interest in the art had waned considerably by the time Freemasonry began to appear, there is still a good chance that these mnemotechnic traditions influenced the original form and purpose of speculative Freemasonry. This paper explores the possible ties between the Craft and the *ars memoria*, and finally shall presents a memory system based on the Renaissance techniques that makes use of modern Masonic symbolism.

The Development of the Art

As the art of memory evolved from its legendary roots into the form used in ancient Rome, classical scholars devised a mnemotechnic system based on their understanding of memory by dividing it into two parts: natural memory and artificial, i.e. trained, memory. The art of memory concerns itself with the development of the latter, and was considered to be a part of classical rhetoric.[1] It continued to be studied and practiced in some form into the European Renaissance, probably falling out of favor with the spread of the printing press and the increased availability of writing materials.

It was during the Renaissance that the art of memory completed its transformation from its presumed classical role as a means to remember facts into a rather mystical discipline.[2]

The art as practiced during the Renaissance took a variety of forms, from the well-known memory palace, to the complex pseudo-kabbalah of Raymond Lull. All of these methods developed the artificial memory as opposed to the natural memory, and most relied heavily on visualization techniques and complex symbolism.

Later methods of the art of memory, such as those described by Giordano Bruno in his works, became extraordinarily complex. Partly because of increased associations with theology, philosophy, and religious magic, and partly because its practice began to be less involved with basic human concerns, it began to be viewed as unworkable and unusable by the average layperson.[3]

Some evidence has been found to suggest that the art of memory was taught and perhaps practiced in historic Masonic lodges. The Second Shaw Statutes, published by William Shaw probably near Holyroodhouse, Scotland,

in 1599, mention that masons were encouraged to practice "the art of memorie and the science thairof." The nature of this wording leads to the conclusion that what is being encouraged is not just the practice of memorization, but that of the Renaissance art of memory.[4] However, unless manuscripts detailing an ancient Masonic

> FROM ITS ROOT as an aid to the rhetorician's art to its Renaissance metamorphosis into a vastly complex mystical science, the *ars memoria* has had a rich and powerful history. It still has great value as a sublime and practical tool for the modern contemplative Freemason.

art of memory are uncovered in the future, the connection between the two will remain merely theoretical. David Stevenson, when examining early catechisms and exposés for signs of a practiced art of memory, finally concludes that "[if] the lodge was indeed a memory temple, it was a crude one, and perhaps much of its significance had been lost in the century since William Shaw had constructed it for the masons."[5]

The Transformative Art of Memory

To understand the esoteric and transformative side of the art of memory, one must first become familiar with some of the beliefs of its practitioners and developers. The art's esoteric practitioners were hermeticists and Neoplatonists. As Neoplatonists, they believed in re-interpretations of many of Plato's core ideas, one such being that the human soul already contained traces and imprints of divine Ideas, and that learning was simply the recollection of those things with which the soul was previously invested before being bound to the world of matter.[6]

They saw the presence of the divine in everything around them and believed that by affixing the images and concepts of these things in the mind that the trained memory became not just a supremely useful tool but a microcosmic reflection of the divine creation.

Modern hermeticism is an intellectual descendant of its Renaissance predecessor, which relied on classical works such as the *Corpus Hermeticum* and contemporary innovations to build a model of the way human consciousness and spirituality interacted with the Universe. Renaissance hermeticists sought to reform man in the image of the Divine through the arts and techniques passed down by classical philosophers.[7] One of the most important elements of this aspect of hermeticism has always been the interplay of the microcosmos and macrocosmos. The Emerald Tablet of Hermes Trismegistus, a medieval hermetic text, famously says, "What is above is like what is below, and what is below is like that which is above, making the miracle of the one thing."[8] This is usually taken to mean that human perfection can be achieved by mirroring the macrocosmos of Creation in the microcosmos of the human form. Renaissance hermeticists searched for means of approaching this sort of human perfection.

The art of memory addresses this problem by developing a practitioner's ability to catalog and contain vast quantities of information within the mind. Through the use of visualization and trained imagination, the practitioner builds a virtual universe within his mind, thus mirroring the macrocosmos within himself. This view of the art of memory could have been encouraged by the *Corpus Hermeticum*. The first book in the collection, titled *Poimandres*, contains this passage:

> He said, "I am the Poimandres [lit., the shepherd of men], the sovereign mind."
>
> I replied, "I wish to understand all things, and grasp the nature of them, and know God. These are the matters I wish to hear about."
>
> He answered, "I know what you wish, and I am with you in every circumstance. Hold in your mind the fullness of what you would know, and I will instruct you."[9]

This highlights the importance of mental mastery in the hermetic philosophy, and thus to the vital role which the art of memory played in the belief system of its Renaissance practitioners.

A Masonic Memory System

As it was explained earlier, if any Masonic art of memory existed in the past, it has been lost. The task of this article is not to attempt to rely on fragmentary, speculative, or fictional Masonic mnemotechnics of early lodges, but instead to draw upon modern ritual and symbolism for inspiration while constructing a new memory system for the contemporary Mason.

We now come to the most important part of this article, the description of a basic Masonic memory system which can be learned, adapted, and built upon by the student. Note that this system is still in its infancy and it is through practice and experimentation that it will be improved and matured until it is a complete and functional *ars memoria*.

While the art of memory takes many forms, one seems particularly suited to Freemasonry. This form, the memory palace, was practiced by forming in the imagination a vast building composed of real or imaginary places, through which the practitioner took an imaginary walk. He would stop at predetermined architectural fixtures called *loci*, or "places," consisting usually of doors, archways, or windows. In each *locus* would be an *imago* (plural *imagines,* pronounced "ee-mah-gin-ayss") or image crafted as a special mnemonic device which would trigger the recollection of a word or idea. It has even been theorized that this sort of imaginary architecture could be the sort of craft which speculative Freemasonry originally involved.[10]

Instead of a memory palace, the Masonic system will use a memory lodge. It too shall use a combination of *loci* and *imagines*, and our next step shall be to lay out the rules for both of these aspects of the memory lodge system.

In a basic memory system, an imago should usually consist of a person engaged in some act or dressed in some way in order to bring to mind the items to remember. In ancient systems, *imagines* normally needed to adhere to certain rules. One rule which was nearly universally present stated that the images should be striking, whether grotesque, hilarious, beautiful, or bizarre. The more striking the image, the more memorable it is apt to be.[11] For example, if one is to remember the three scents, laurel, frankincense, and myrrh, one might form an image of Stan Laurel (of Laurel and Hardy fame) looking into a mirror and admiring his big, green, monstrous nose. Mr. Laurel, of course, would remind one of laurel. The word "mirror" sounds much like "myrrh", helping to remember the second scent, and the big green nose came from Frankenstein's monster, which would help one remember "frankincense."

One may wince and groan at the horrible puns, but one is also not likely to forget the association between Frankenstein's monster's nose and frankincense. The picture formed is a strange one, and its bizarre qualities adequately fulfill that basic rule for images.

Masonic *imagines* should follow this basic rule. They should be strikingly memorable. However, there are two other important rules for our memory images. First, the images should utilize as many Masonic symbols as possible. In its rich symbolism, Freemasonry already contains dozens of suitable elements which can be used to create vivid and memorable images. What's more, the esoteric or contemplative Mason has already attached special and personal meanings to many of its symbols. Using these in an art of memory and attaching additional meanings to them can open the doors to new revelations and understandings. Because these meanings and associations are meant to be powerful and moving, the second additional rule for our Masonic memory system is that Masonic symbols should not be associated with concepts or ideas which run contrary to their meanings in a derogatory or negative manner.

Let us now turn our attention to the second essential element of our memory system: its *loci*, or places. These too should be distinctive and easy to remember, but as they are reused over and over again they are more easily fixed in the mind and need not be so striking and bizarre as the *imagines*. There are two types of *loci*. The first type are imaginary places, and while our basic memory lodge will not utilize any imaginary places, suggestions for advanced methods using imaginary memory places will be presented later. The second type of *loci* are real places which have been carefully observed and remembered by the practitioner. Our memory lodge will be constructed using real places located in a real lodge.

Begin by imagining the lodge room with which you are most familiar. The process of creating a memory lodge is probably easier if you are actually standing in the lodge room as you are committing it to memory. You should mentally walk around the room, beginning at the door to the preparation room and continuing clockwise along the north, east, south, and west sides of the lodge, then proceeding and finally stopping at the altar. At every officer's station, mentally stop and turn to look at the station, and imagine yourself saluting the station with the due guard and penal sign of an Entered Apprentice. As each station will become one of your *loci*, it needs to be sharp, clear, and well-lit, and should be large enough to hold roughly one person. Try not to clutter the *loci* together too closely, skipping some stations if needed.

As lodge room layouts vary by jurisdiction, use the pattern with which you are most familiar. You should be able to fit eight to ten stations easily in your memory lodge. You may want to add one *locus* just inside the preparation room door, and a second at the altar.

Once the memory lodge has been constructed in your mind, mentally walk through it two or three times, slowly and methodically. Take note of the furniture and decorations of the lodge and remember to salute each station as you turn to examine it.

Using the Memory Lodge

Frequent practice is required to make this memory system usable. At first, you should simply devote 10–15 minutes per day to simply walking through your memory lodge. After several days of this, you should begin working on memorizing something. Begin by memorizing something short and Masonic. Before beginning to memorize using your new memory lodge, it is important to understand the difference between the memorization of things, and the memorization of words. Memorizing a list of things, such as a grocery list, is straightforward. One simply creates an image for each thing in the list, and stores one image in each *locus* in order. Memorizing words, such as a lecture or body of text, is slightly more difficult and requires more practice. One might attempt to memorize an image for every word, but it is easy to see that this is impractical. When memorizing words, most may find it easier to break the text up into small, manageable chunks. Each of these chunks would be memorized by rote and associated with an image whose characteristics could serve to bring the piece of text to mind. For example, when memorizing the teaching that a Mason is divested of all metallic substances for three reasons, one might create a memory image of a man carrying a wooden sword with a numeral three painted conspicuously on his chest. The wooden sword would serve as a reminder of the metallic substances he's not carrying, and the big three would be a reminder of the number of reasons. The rest would need to be memorized by rote.

The following list contains suggestions of various Masonic topics and exercises that one could use to practice memorization using a memory lodge.

- The Ancient Landmarks make a good starting point. There may be too many to fit in your memory lodge, so perhaps starting with just the first ten would work. Some of the shorter lectures in the degree rituals should fit in your memory lodge. The apron lecture or the "G" lecture are excellent candidates for this type of memorization.

MASTERS CARPET

- After moving on to the advanced methods described below, memorize the full degree lectures using the memory lodge system—the Middle Chamber lecture is in fact already in that format.
- Integrate the Tracing Boards or similar illustrations into your memory lodge. Also, the so-called "Master's Carpet," a classic American Masonic engraving from J. L. Cross' *True Masonic Chart* (1819, image reproduced on p. 67) might form a useful starting point.
- Reflect on the old teaching from William Preston's lecture that "objects which particularly strike the eye will more immediately engage the attention, and imprint on the memory serious and solemn truths."[12]
- Use the memory lodge to memorize non-Masonic things using Masonic symbols. Observe how you choose to map the profane world into the Masonic world.
- Explore other memory systems, such as Bro∴ John Michael Greer's "memory garden."[13]

Finally, experiment. The art of memory has been neglected for centuries and is just now beginning to gain attention from the Masonic community. So much has been lost or forgotten that we really don't know what's possible, so try different techniques and share what you learn.

Additional Methods

After a month or so of using your memory lodge, it will become apparent that ten *loci* just isn't enough. Below are some suggestions for advanced methods that one can use to expand his Masonic memory system. Many of these suggestions involve combinations of real and imaginary *loci*, which will be treading on new ground. Some of the old memory treatises caution the practitioner against using imaginary places, but others mention mixing the two with no loss in effectiveness.[14] It could be that the effectiveness of imaginary memory places is tied to the amount of effort and detail given to them.

MEMORY OCTAGON

The first advanced method provides an imaginary space for storing up to eight memory lodges. To use it, imagine yourself in a large octagonal hall. The floor is checkered with white and black tiles, and in the center of the floor is a blazing star. Overhead, the arched ceiling, lit by elegant lamps in the eight corners of the room, is painted to match the starry sky. Each of the eight walls contains two doors, and each set of doors leads to a lodge room.

These lodge rooms should each be real lodges that one has committed to memory. Each time one finds himself needing a new set of *loci*, a new lodge should be visited and committed to memory in the same manner as the first basic memory lodge.

WINDING STAIRCASE

The second technique is even more difficult, and requires more rote memory work than the first. This technique uses the Fellow Craft "staircase" lecture to create a memory system, utilizing the rich symbolism of the winding staircase to decorate and differentiate the *loci*. Because this memory staircase will consist entirely of imaginary places, it may require more effort on the practitioner's part to use effectively.

First, devise a way to link the staircase to your existing memory structure. This author

Figure 1: A Masonic visual alphabet

A	Altar	J	the Holy Sts. John	S	Tiler's sword
B	Beehive	K	King Solomon	T	Temple of Solomon
C	Cable-Tow	L	Level	V	Square
D	Due Guard	M	Setting-maul	W	the Waterford (Jordan)
E	47th problem of Euclid	N	Network (of the Pillars)	X	Scythe
F	Blazing Star (five points)	O	Point within a Circle	Y	Hourglass
G	Gavel	P	Pavement	Z	Coffin
H	Highest Hill	Q	Quarry		
I	Plumb	R	Noah's ark		

has found it useful to devote one wall of the memory octagon to the staircase doors. Note that these doors should be flanked by the two brazen pillars, which, when fitted with alcoves, provide the first two imaginary *loci*. One should focus on all of the details of these pillars, from their massive size to the ornate chapiters. As one passes between the pillars and begin to climb the staircase, each stair should be large enough to hold an archway or pedestal decorated with the symbols for that stair.

For example, the first stair could have a pedestal decorated with a young man holding a plumb. Each step on the staircase provides a new *locus*. While these imaginary places may require a great deal of work and memorization to initially create, they also provide the perfect memory system in which to store the second degree lecture.

At the end of the staircase, one may then place an entirely new octagon filled with entirely new memory lodges. Each of these should operate on the Fellow Craft degree, meaning that when they are created and used, the stations therein should be hailed using that degree's due guard and penal sign instead of those belonging to the Entered Apprentice. It may even be possible to re-use the lodges from the first memory octogon, with all of the changes in furniture pursuant to the Fellow Craft degree.

CONCORDANT BODIES

The concordant bodies provide a plethora of additional lodge layouts, rituals, and symbol sets. For instance, by linking together all of the degrees and lodge rooms of the Scottish Rite, one would be able to create a memory system of roughly 300 *loci* even without utilizing the memory octagons described earlier. As most Masons have not had the opportunity to see all thirty-three of the Scottish Rite degrees, much of this technique would also rely on a combination of imaginary and real places.

MEMORY ALPHABETS

Some Medieval memory systems used visual alphabets to aid in the recollection of specific words and phrases. With these alphabets, each letter is represented by a symbol or image that resembles it, or by animals or birds arranged in alphabetical order, one for each letter of the alphabet.[15] There are enough Masonic symbols to provide such an alphabet, and one example is given in Figure 1. This visual alphabet would be committed to memory using standard rote memorization, and the symbols could then be used to augment memory images. For example, if one wished to remember that a particular image had to do with brotherly love, relief, and truth, one would incorporate a beehive, Noah's ark, and a twenty-four inch gauge into the image to serve as a mnemonic for the first letter of each of the items. Old tracing boards and ritual monitors are great sources for visual alphabet images. Allen E. Roberts' *The Craft and Its Symbols* contains artwork for nearly every symbol presented in all three of the Blue Lodge degrees. W. Kirk MacNulty's lavish *Freemasonry: Symbols, Secrets, Significance* contains hundreds of useful images. And Julian Rees' *Tracing Boards of the Three Degree of Craft Freemasonry Explained* is the ultimate resource for tracing board images. [See the *Ahiman* review of Rees' book in this volume, pp. 127–31.—Ed.]

Conclusion

From its roots as an aid to the rhetorician's art to its Renaissance metamorphosis into a vastly complex mystical science, the *ars memoria* has had a rich and powerful history. The Craft's common ground with the art of memory suggests that it still has great value as a sublime and practical tool for the modern contemplative Freemason. ✦

Notes

1. Frances A. Yates, *The Art of Memory* (Chicago: University of Chicago Press, 1966), 20.
2. For a detailed survey of the subject in general, see the article by Thomas D. Worrel in this volume of *Ahiman* (pp. 30–61).
3. John Hale, *The Civilization of Europe in the Renaissance* (New York: Atheneum, 1994), 208.
4. David Stevenson, *The Origins of Freemasonry: Scotland's Century, 1590–1710* (Cambridge, UK: Cambridge University Press, 1988), 44–49.
5. Ibid., 140–42.
6. For a summary of Neoplatonism, see Paulina Remes, *Neoplatonism* (Berkeley, Calif.: University of California Press, 2008.).
7. Giovanni Pico della Mirandola, *Oration on the Dignity of Man*, (Washington, D.C.: Regnery Gateway, 1956), xiii–xvi.
8. Tabula Smaragdina, line 1 (*Quod est inferius est sicut quod est superius, et quod est superius est sicut quod est inferius, ad perpetranda miracula rei unius.*). Compare the early Christian writing, *Odes of Solomon*: "The likeness of that which is below is that which is on high." (34:4)
9. *Poimandres* 1.10–15 (trans. by Shawn Eyer).
10. Yates, *Art of Memory*, 294.
11. Ibid., 25–28.
12. Colin F. W. Dyer, *William Preston and His Work* (Shepperton, UK: Lewis Masonic, 1987), 189.
13. John Michael Greer, "Ars Memorativa: An Introduction to the Hermetic Art of Memory," *Caduceus, The Hermetic Quarterly* 1 (Summer 1995):2.
14. Yates, *Art of Memory*, 24, 75, 316–17.
15. Yates, *Art of Memory*, 124–27.

A Lodge Salutatory · *Robert G. Davis*

Come, Comrades!
With others gathered in secret place.
In voices greeting, and ancient prayer;
Kindred brothers of bright inheritance.
Joined with others chosen;
all friends of Mason's square.

Come, Friends!
Each bound by sacred vows
In hand and heart; all brothers bright.
Sworn in truth in Masons' house
Where the darkest soul finds light.

Come, Fellows!
Together in mind, in word, and deed
Each linked by solemn ties and duty
With one and all; in fraternal bond agreed
To build a Temple of wisdom, strength, and beauty.

Come, Craftsmen!
Clothed in aprons white
On holy journey to eternity.
Each seeking Masons' Light
From the mantle of sacred fraternity.

Come, Brethren!
All pledged in deep accord
To that universal love within.
Sing Masonry's praise, with heart and word.
All hail! Our mystic brotherhood of men.

The Allegory of the Cave

Plato

> Plato's famous allegory of the cave, written around 380 BCE, is one of the
> most important and influential passages of *The Republic*. It vividly illustrates
> the concept of Idealism as it was taught in the Platonic Academy, and provides
> a metaphor which philosophers have used for milennia to help us overcome
> superficiality and materialism. In this dialogue, Socrates (the main speaker)
> explains to Plato's brother, Glaukon, that we all resemble captives who are
> chained deep within a cavern, who do not yet realize that there is more to
> reality than the shadows they see against the wall.

AND NOW ALLOW ME to draw a comparison in order to understand the effect of learning (or the lack thereof) upon our nature. Imagine that there are people living in a cave deep underground. The cavern has a mouth that opens to the light above, and a passage exists from this all the way down to the people.

They have lived here from infancy, with their legs and necks bound in chains. They cannot move. All they can do is stare directly forward, as the chains stop them from turning their heads around. Imagine that far above and behind them blazes a great fire. Between this fire and the captives, a low partition is erected along a path, something like puppeteers use to conceal themselves during their shows.

GLAUKON: I can picture it.

SOCRATES: Look and you will also see other people carrying objects back and forth along the partition, 514c things of every kind: images of people 515a and animals, carved in stone and wood and other materials. Some of these other people speak, while others remain silent.

GLAUKON: A bizarre situation for some unusual captives.

◄ Ascending to the exit of an ancient cistern in Mycenae, Greece.
Photo by Domenico Pellegriti, 2009.

SOCRATES: So we are! Now, tell me if you suppose it's possible that these captives ever saw anything of themselves or one another, other than the shadows flitting across the cavern wall before them?

GLAUKON: Certainly not, for they are restrained, [515b] all their lives, with their heads facing forward only.

SOCRATES: And that would be just as true for the objects moving to and fro behind them?

GLAUKON: Certainly.

SOCRATES: Now, if they could speak, would you say that these captives would imagine that the names they gave to the things they were able to see applied to real things?

GLAUKON: It would have to be so.

SOCRATES: And if a sound reverberated through their cavern from one of those others passing behind the partition, do you suppose that the captives would think anything but the passing shadow was what really made the sound?

GLAUKON: No, by Zeus.

SOCRATES: [515c] Then, undoubtedly, such captives would consider the truth to be nothing but the shadows of the carved objects.

GLAUKON: Most certainly.

SOCRATES: Look again, and think about what would happen if they were released from these chains and these misconceptions. Imagine one of them is set free from his shackles and immediately made to stand up and bend his neck around, to take steps, to gaze up toward the fire. And all of this was painful, and the glare from the light made him unable to see the objects that cast the shadows he once beheld. [515d] What do you think his reaction would be if someone informed him that everything he had formerly known was illusion and delusion, but that now he was a few steps closer to reality, oriented now toward things that were more authentic, and able to see more truly? And, even further, if one would direct his attention to the artificial figures passing to and fro and ask him what their names are, would this man not be at a loss to do so? Would he, rather, believe that the shadows he formerly knew were more real than the objects now being shown to him?

GLAUKON: Much more real.

SOCRATES: Now, if he was forced to look directly at the firelight, [515e] wouldn't his eyes be pained? Wouldn't he turn away and run back to those things which he normally perceived and understand them as more defined and clearer than the things now being brought to his attention?

GLAUKON: That's right.

SOCRATES: Now, let's say that he is forcibly dragged up the steep climb out of the cavern, and firmly held until finally he stands in the light of the sun. Don't you think that he would be agitated and even begin to complain? [516a] Under that light, would his eyes not be nearly blinded, unable to discern any of those things that we ourselves call real?

GLAUKON: No, he wouldn't see them at first.

SOCRATES: It would take time, I suppose, for him to get used to seeing higher things. In the beginning, he might only trace the shadows. Then, reflections of people and other things in the water. Next he would come to see the things themselves. Then he would behold the heavenly bodies, and the heaven itself by night, seeing the light [516b] of the stars and the moon with greater ease than the sun and its light by day.

GLAUKON: Indeed so.

SOCRATES: And then, I think, he would at last be able to gaze upon the sun itself—neither as reflected in water, nor as a phantom image in some other place, but in its own place as it really is.

GLAUKON: Undeniably.

SOCRATES: And now, he will begin to reason. He will find that the sun is the source for the seasons and the years, and governor of every visible thing, [516c] and is ultimately the origin of everything previously known.

GLAUKON: Of course. First he would see and then draw conclusions.

SOCRATES: That being the case, should he remember his fellow prisoners and their original dwelling and what was accepted as wisdom in that setting, don't you imagine he would consider himself fortunate for this transformation, and feel pity for the captives?

GLAUKON: I agree.

SOCRATES: Now…suppose there were honors and awards among the captives, which they granted as prizes to one another for being the best at recognizing the various shadows passing by or deciphering their patterns, 516d their order, and the relationships among them, and therefore best at predicting what shadow would be seen next. Do you believe that our liberated man would be much concerned with such honors, or that he would be jealous of those who received them? Or that he would strive to be like those who were lauded by the captives and enjoyed pride of place among them? Or would rather take Homer's view, and "rather wish, in earthly life, to be the humble serf of a landless man" (*Odyssey* 11.489) and suffer whatever he had to, instead of holding the views of the captives and returning to that state of being?

GLAUKON: 516e Truly, he would rather suffer a great deal than return to such a life.

SOCRATES: Well, here's something else to consider. If such a man would suddenly go from the sunlight to once more descend to his original circumstances, wouldn't his vision by obscured by the darkness?

GLAUKON: It obviously would.

SOCRATES: And so, let's say he is with the captives and gets put into the position 517a of interpreting the wall-shadows. His eyes are still adjusting to the darkness, and it may take a while before they are. Wouldn't he become a laughing-stock? Wouldn't they say, "You have returned from your adventure up there with ruined eyes!" Would they not say that the ascent was a waste of time? And if they had the opportunity, do you supposed that they might raise their hands against him and kill this person who is trying to liberate them to a higher plane?"

GLAUKON: I'm afraid so.

SOCRATES: Then, my friend Glaukon, this image applies to everything we've been discussing. 517b It compares the visible world to the underground cavern, and the power of the sun to the fire that burned in the cavern. You won't misunderstand me if you connect the captive's ascent to be the ascent of the soul to the intellible world (τὸν νοητὸν τόπον). This is how I believe, and I shared it at your wish, though heaven knows whether it is at all true. Regardless, it appears to me that in the realm what what can be known, 517c the Idea of the Good is discovered last of all, and it only perceived with great difficulty. But, when it is seen, it leads us directly to the finding that it is the universal cause of all that is right and beautiful. It is the source of visible light and the master of the same, and in the intelligible world it is the master of truth and reason. And whoever, in private or in public, would behave in a sensible way, will keep this idea in focus.

GLAUKON: I agree. to the extent I can manage to understand.

SOCRATES: Stay with me, then, for another thought. We should not be surprised that individuals who have reached this level might be unwilling to spend their time on mundane affairs, for would it not be that their souls always feel a calling to the higher things. [517d] If our illustration holds true, that would seem quite likely.

GLAUKON: Yes, likely indeed.

SOCRATES: Now, would it be at all surprising for one who has been engaged in the contemplation of holy things, when he ventures into ways of degenerate humanity, to appear ridiculous in his actions? What if, for example, while his eyes were still adjusting to the mundane gloom, he would be forced to appear in court to hold forth about the mere shadows of justice or the other shapes that flitted across the wall? And to engage in debate [517e] about such concepts with the minds of others who has never beheld the Ideal Justice?

GLAUKON: It would not surprise me the least.

SOCRATES:[518a] But one who has his wits about him would remember that there are two things that pain the eyes: being brought from darkness to light, and transitioning back from light to darkness. Now, considering that the soul experiences the same discomfort, this man would not make light of another when he met with a confused soul. He would take the time to understand if that soul was coming from a luminous realm and his eyes were blinded by darkness, or [518b] whether journeying from the darkness of ignorance into an illuminated state had overwhelmed his eyes. One, he would consider fortunate. He would pity the other—and if he laughed at either, it would be less justified if he laughed at the expense of the one who was descending from the light above.

GLAUKON: That's a fitting way to put it.

SOCRATES: Of course, if I'm correct, then some of our educators are mistaken in their view that it is possible to implant knowledge into a person that wasn't there originally, like vision into the eyes of a blind man.

GLAUKON: That's what they say.

SOCRATES: What our message now signifies is that the ability and means of learning is already present in the soul. As the eye could not turn from darkness to light unless the whole body moved, so it is that the mind can only turn around from the world of becoming to that of Being by a movement of the whole soul. The soul must learn, by degrees, to endure the contemplation of Being and the luminous realms. This is the Good, agreed?

GLAUKON: 518d Agreed.

SOCRATES: Therefore, of this matter itself, there must be a craft of some kind, which would be a most efficient and effective means of transforming the soul. It would not be an art that gives the soul vision, but a craft at labor under the assumption that the soul has its own innate vision, but does not apply it properly. There must be some kind of means for bringing this about.

GLAUKON: Yes. Such a craft must exist. ⚔

Masonic Initiation
& Plato's Allegory of the Cave

David E. Stafford

> Masonry...tends to create a new people, which, composed of men of many nations and tongues, shall all be bound together by the bonds of science, morality, and virtue. [...] It is philosophical, because it teaches the great Truths concerning the nature and existence of one Supreme Deity, and the existence and immortality of the soul. It revives the Academe of Plato, and the wise teachings of Socrates.
>
> Albert Pike

THROUGHOUT HISTORY there have been many men who have attained a stature of high regard in the halls of Freemasonry. These men were usually individuals who had a great positive effect upon the world about them, whether socially, academically, philosophically, or Masonically. These are men who embraced enlightenment. One such man is the great philosophical teacher, Plato. In the writings of Bro∴ Albert Pike, Plato's time-honored teachings are cited repeatedly. Several lessons from this great educator's repertoire have parallels to the system of Freemasonry. One of them, Plato's Allegory of the Cave, recorded in the seventh book of *The Republic*, should have great Masonic significance for all who have been initiated into the Craft.

Before undertaking the task of exploring the parallels between Freemasonry and Plato's Allegory of the Cave, it is prudent to examine what, if any, connection Plato has with the Craft and its development. First and foremost, it is important to assert, at the onset of this exploration, that there will be no claim that Plato was inducted into the mysteries of Freemasonry or that it traces its lineage from his, or any other, ancient mystery school. This examination will only look at what the shapers and formers of modern Freemasonry thought about and gleaned from Plato's writings and example. Any obvious connections that can be drawn between Plato's Allegory of the Cave and the modern institution of Free and Accepted Masonry will also be reviewed.

Plato's Life and Academy

Although there is some debate as to the date of Plato's birth, it is generally accepted that he was born around the year 428 BCE.[1] His given name was Aristocles. The name Plato was seemingly a nickname meaning broad, perhaps in reference to his physical appearance. Plato's early life is blurred by antiquity and unreliable accounts. His immediate family was politically connected and affluent, and Plato most likely lived an early life of little difficulty.

Perhaps the most influential experience in Plato's life was the death of his revered teacher, Socrates. Plato was twenty-eight when Socrates was condemned to death by drinking the notorious hemlock.[2] Following Socrates' death, Plato left Athens and traveled to Megara, Cyrene, Italy, Sicily, and Egypt. It is during this time of travel that Plato sought initiation into the Egyptian Mysteries but was rejected by the high priest. "You Greeks are but children in the secret doctrine," Sais, the priest, was reported to have replied to Plato's requests to being inducted into the mysteries there.[3] But we know from the dialogues that, despite this, Socrates, Plato and others in their intellectual environment had a strong background in the Greek mystery traditions: the Eleusinian and Dionysian initiations are particularly emphasized.

Following his travels and search for intellectual and spiritual light, Plato returned to Athens around the age of forty, and he established a school, the Academy, in the Grove of Academus.[4] Plato's school was geographically located within a grove or a public park filled with gymnasia, altars, statues, and temples.

Plato's Academy most probably was a loose connection of men who came to learn criticism of method by listening to his dialogues and in-struction. The leader or head of the Academy was elected for life by the majority vote of its members. Plato remained the Head of the Academy until his death in 348/347 BCE. It was in the Academy that Plato instructed some of the greatest intellectual minds of Western civilization, including Aristotle.

Masonic Writers and Plato

Albert Pike, who incidentally was called by some the "Plato of Freemasonry," held the teachings of Plato in high esteem.[5] In *Morals and Dogma*, Pike reveals his position that Plato is among the greatest revelers of truth and light.[6] Pike offers the view that Plato expounded and expressed the noble doctrine of nature "in the most beautiful and luminous manner."[7]

Wilmshurst refers to Plato in his classic work, *The Meaning of Masonry*. Wilmshurst stated that in order to fully understand the Fellow Craft degree, a student of Freemasonry must study two ancient sources. The first of these is Plato's dialogues, the other, the "records of the classical Christian contemplatives."[8] Of interest is Wilmshurst's reminder to the reader that Plato refers to the four cardinal virtues in the *Phaedo* and the Book of Wisdom 8:5–7. If the studying Mason researches this point, he will not find the familiar Masonic virtues of fortitude, prudence, temperance, and justice. Instead he would find justice, temperance, wisdom, and courage.

As Mackey's *Symbolism of Freemasonry* relates, "Plato says that the design of initiation was to restore the soul to that state of perfection from which it had originally fallen."[9] This being taken from the *Phaedo*, it is evident the general esoteric goal of both the ancient mysteries and modern Freemasonry are similar in concept.

The Dionysian Artificers, writen in 1820 by

Hippolyto da Costa (a student of William Preston), refers to Plato numerous times. The work points out the importance of understanding that fables and allegories often contain numerous meanings, and alludes to "the general doctrine of Plato of the descent of the soul into the darkness; of the body, the perils of the passions, the torments of vices."[10]

The Allegory of the Cave

In Plato's Allegory of the Cave, human prisoners are held captive deep in the earth.[11] Their necks and ankles chained, they have never seen the outside world, the sun, or each other. They are bound facing a stone wall. Behind the captives is a fire, and in front of the fire a walkway on which men carry puppets and items from the outside world. These items include statues of gods, men, animals, and trees. The firelight casts shadows of them upon the cavern wall— the captives are only able to see these flitting shadows. The bondsmen have no understanding of their condition: their world is made up only of the illusions of distorted shadows cast upon the stone wall before them. The sounds and voices heard by those kept enslaved are only echoes and reverberations from the outside. As they sit in darkness, their reality is limited and their morals only based on their own understandings of distorted truths and skewed sounds from the outside world.

The allegory continues to explain that the prisoners cling to their own prejudices and self-conceived notions of reality. Plato asserts that if all the prisoners were released to turn and see the elements that created their reality, the prisoners would be blinded by the light of the fire. The prisoners, according to Plato, would quickly become angered by what they viewed and desire to return to their shackled condition.

However, Plato suggests that if only one prisoner had his chains removed, the response would be vastly different. The prisoner would turn to see the fire, the walk way, and the other prisoners bound in a blind state. The allegory continues with the prisoner being dragged out of the cave and presented to the sunlit world outside. There he sees that the realities and morals of his world are only an illusion. Plato believed a return to the cave would be almost impossible because the prisoner would have seen his previously darkened condition as an enslaved state.

AN INITIAL EXAMINATION

In the centuries between Plato's first oration of this described allegory and today, there have been countless interpretations of its meaning. Its ability to be interpreted in varied ways makes it such a fundamental and enduring legacy of the thoughts and teachings of Plato. Why then should it not be appropriate to ascertain a Masonic interpretation of Plato's Allegory of the Cave?

In *From Socrates to Sartre: The Philosophic Quest*, Dr. T. Z. Lavine of George Washington University, describes the allegory in a manner that one could use to describe the Craft itself:

> It is an allegory of our time as needing to be born again, to emerge from the darkness of corruption into the light of truth and morality. It is an educational allegory of our time as needing to ascend through stages of education from the darkness of intellectual and moral confusion in its everyday beliefs, to the light of true knowledge and values.[12]

Lavine's brief interpretations of the allegory provide a springboard for its analysis in terms of Masonic tradition.

A late Renaissance engraving titled *Antrum Platonicum* by Jan Saenredam, 1604, after a lost painting by Cornelis Cornelisz. Plato's Allegory of the Cave is vividly interpreted, with an emphasis upon a community of philosophers who are actively engaged in the liberation of the captives—what Plato referred to as "the craft of turning souls around."

Freemasonry hopes to lead its initiates to higher understandings of truth and life to put away the dim light of superstition and passion to embrace the illumination of reason, intellectual knowledge, and immutable values.

Both Freemasonry and Plato's allegory begin with men in a darkened condition. The men in the cave are groping in darkness and bound to the blighted beliefs of superstition and self-prescribed truths. It is noteworthy to point out that the allegory takes place within a cave. Caverns have long been considered, Masonically, to be "a symbol of the darkness of ignorance and crime impenetrable to the light of truth."[13] In the ninth degree of the Scottish Rite, "the cave is a symbol of the imprisonment of the human soul and intellect by ignorance, superstition, deceit, and fraud."[14] One who has petitioned for the degrees of Freemasonry and awaits his initiation is held in the bondage of ignorance

just as the mass of mankind is held in ignorance to the great and true teachings of the Craft. "There disinterestedness vanishes, every one howls, searches, gropes, and gnaws for himself. Ideas are ignored, and of progress there is no thought."[15] Just as the profane is satisfied by the broken image of himself, so are the individuals in the cave content with living in darkness without any hope of intellectual growth or true fulfillment. It is also noteworthy to point out that the three ruffians, in the Ninth degree, are found hiding in a cave. Where else do ignorance, tyranny, and fanaticism belong?

In his allegory, Plato presents with a very interesting assertion. He presents an occurrence where all the prisoners are released to turn and see the images within the cave. As they view the darkness around them, their eyes are not able to adjust to the protruding and offensive brightness of the fire's light. They quickly become disillusioned and repulsed by the image and desire to return to their once darkened condition.

Does this image not hold great Masonic meaning? The shackled prisoners represent the mass of mankind. In *Morals and Dogma*, Bro∴ Pike states that "people, as a mass, [are] rude and unorganized."[16] Mankind, as an innate passion, loves squalor and ignorance. It is only through the instruction of an agent, such as Freemasonry, that the individual, not the mass, can be raised above his inborn breeding and grow intellectually. All men are not suited for the secret teachings of the Craft. They are unable to grasp its rich meaning and hidden gems of purpose. It is only the few, the minority of intellectually prone individuals, who can be lifted up from the mire of mankind's filth to be bettered by the teachings of the Craft. The mass would be unable to perceive the teachings of the allegories of Masonry and would quickly be blinded and wish to return to their previous status in life. As the Hebrew proverb states, "As a dog returneth to his vomit, so a fool returneth to his folly." (Proverbs 26:11) Freemasonry has always known that the masses are not compatible with its teachings; therefore, it has only intended to admit the finest individuals of society into the progressive course of instruction it has to offer.

THE ALLEGORY IN TERMS OF MASONIC INITIATION

The degrees of the Craft are only represented within Plato's allegory when considering the individual, just as only one man should be introduced to the mysteries of Masonry at a time. The uninitiated is hoodwinked and blinded to the occurrences about him. He is kept in darkness for two reasons. The first reason is a reminder of the vow of secrecy soon to be taken.

Secondly, it is intended that the candidate for the Entered Apprentice degree, and all others, perceive the forms of the Lodge *in his heart* before he views the beauties thereof with his eyes. The individual in Plato's allegory is kept in darkness to reality. During this time, he uses shadows and distorted noises to conceive the reality that is around him, and the proselyte is not brought to light until after his cable tow has been removed. In the allegory, the prisoner is not brought to light until his shackles are opened. The agent who brings him to initial light walks him around the cave and points to objects and demands the individual to name them. The parallel exists that neither the individual released from bondage nor the newly made brother within the lodge are brought to complete light. The teachings of both are only partial. The two initiates are allowed to adjust to the new light that has been shown them and expected to progress through further stages to attain more light and greater understanding.

The next development in the journey of a man seeking Masonic enlightenment occurs through the teachings and philosophy of the Fellow Craft degree. This second degree of Masonry is filled with great and enduring ideas and teachings for the neophyte seeking further light in the Craft. The legend of the winding staircase holds lessons of the utmost importance, and within its beautifully illustrated lessons lie one word that most suitably expresses its meaning. That single word is ascension. The passage taken to the Holy of Holies is sacred and dominated by the ascension of a winding staircase. This winding staircase is symbolic of the journey of one seeking a liberal education. Mackey explains, "the path of the Fellow Craft requires him to ascend, step by step, until he has reached the summit, where the treasures of knowledge await him."[17]

The Allegory of *The Bird*
by Abū ʿAlī al-Ḥusayn ibn ʿAbd Allāh ibn Sīnāʾ (980–1037 CE)

HAVING BEEN ensnared by a group of hunters and locked up in a cage, the Souls of mortals, like a swarm of captive birds, refuse to accept fate and struggle for release. Only a few of them, however, are fortunate enough to escape, with parts of their shackles still clinging to their claws. The others are left behind but are eventually rescued by their companions.

They set out together in search of safety on the top of the eight-story Mountain of God. As they reached the seventh story they settle down to rest in the midst of green pastures and flowing streams.

They are soon roused to a new sense of urgency and head for the eight story, where they come upon a species of bird the like of which, in beauty, sweetness and affability, they had never seen before. Before long, the bonds of friendship between them have grown so strong that the hosts are only too glad now to lead their guests to the city of the Great King, before whom they would lay their burdens.

But as soon as their eyes fall on the radiant countenance of the King, they are infatuated. As they enumerate their grievances, the Great King listens sympathetically, promises them complete resistution of liberty, and bids them go in peace.

And so they go, with the most vivid impression of that vision of beauty whose enjoyments brings supreme happiness, and the conviction that never again will they be able to feel quite at home in that "vale of sorrow" from which they originally came.

Majid Fakhry, *A History of Islamic Philosophy*.
New York: Columbia University Press, 2004, pp. 161–62.

Education is the great equalizer and is the one thing that a man can do to elevate himself above others. H. L. Haywood stresses the second degree's importance in elevating men intellectually. All men who seek elevation are destined to ascend the enlightened path of knowledge. Education and academics are the paths by which Masonry teaches one must take to truly find enlightenment.[18]

The experience of the freedman, within Plato's allegory, being dragged from the darkness of the cave can be compared to the winding staircase of the second degree. It is through this ascending passage that he finds the most brilliant light.

An apparent contradiction between the allegory and the second degree is the fact that the individual in the allegory is "forcibly dragged up the steep climb out of the cavern, and firmly held until finally he stands in the light of the sun."[19] Freemasonry never forces itself upon initiates. It is through one's own freewill and accord that an individual is exposed to the teachings of the Craft. However, many of us have had the experience, long after initiation, of suddenly "seeing more" in the symbolism than we did at first. And it can even be a painful experience, if what we see grieves our conscience, or challenges us to improve ourselves in ways that will not be easy.

When Plato's captive approaches the light, "would his eyes not be nearly blinded, unable to discern any of those things that we ourselves call real?"[20] This passage is true for both the allegory and the newly passed Fellow Craft. In each degree of Freemasonry, the brilliant light to which the candidate is exposed is so bright he at first is blinded by it. This may be symbolically represented by the traditional requirement of a waiting and studying period between degrees. In some Lodges, the period can be as long as a

Detail of William Tringham's 1755 Masonic engraving, *Hieroglyphica*. The imagery seems directly inspired by Plato's allegory of the cave. The Worshipful Master of a lodge is shown at the mouth of a cave, surrounded by his officers. Above them, the celestial bodies and archetypal world appears. The figure of divine Wisdom holds a scroll with the Latin motto *Hic Labor Hoc Opus*, "This is the task, this is the work." It is drawn from a passage in Virgil's *Aeneid*: "The way into the underworld is easy; the gates of darkness are ever wide. But to ascend back out, to retrace our steps to the air above...that's the task, the work" (6.126)

year, and a lecture is required before advancement might be made. This period allows maturation and ample reflection upon the seeds sewn within the lessons of the degree.

It is through the maturation of a candidate spiritually and intellectually, his listening to the instruction of well informed brethren, and the reflection upon the lessons taught him that a man is prepared to experience the life changing episode of the third degree of Masonry. Only after a candidate has first been brought to light and shown the initial beauties of the lodge and passed through the ascension of growth intellectually that a man can be raised to the newness of life as a Master Mason. The same journey, symbolically and allegorically, had to occur to the released prisoner. He had to first be brought to the understanding that he was in a state of bondage. After which, he was caused to pass through the ascension of knowledge to seek the bright light at the pinnacle of the summit. It is at this summit that the *free man* is brought to full illumination and entitled to freely see the realities of the world about him.

It would take time...for him to get used to seeing higher things. In the beginning, he might only trace the shadows. Then, reflections of people and other things in the water. Next he would come to see the things themselves. Then he would behold the heavenly bodies, and the heaven itself by night, seeing the light of the stars and the moon with greater ease than the sun and its light by day. And then…he would at last be able to gaze upon the sun itself—neither as reflected in water, nor as a phantom image in some other place, but *in its own place as it really is.*[21]

Through the lessons of the third degree a man is shown his place in the world as an immortal being destined to be resurrected by the ultimate Creator. The teachings of the third degree are explained to the newly raised brother; however, the truer and deeper realities and meanings of the degree are much later discovered, if ever. The freed prisoner in Plato's allegory is able to view all the glories of the real world once he has completed his ascent from the cave; so as, the Master Mason is entitled and does receive a full explanation of the mysteries of Craft Masonry. Neither individual is at once able to comprehend the beauties he is caused to behold. It is through the reflection and consistent study upon what is seen and experienced that the true lessons are learned by both.

The Allegory of the Cave illustrates "the significance of free and independent thought as a pathway to truth."[22] Thus, the prisoner who first escaped "from the cave of deceptive shadows and discovered reality is someone who has learned Masonic truth."[23]

Plato taught the things we see, touch, smell, and hear are not the ultimate reality. Plato believed that all that we perceive with our senses must be elevated through the mind before true understanding can occur. It was, according to Plato, the role of the philosopher to help others release the light within his students to allow them to understand the world around them through a stimulated mind.

Many of our most distinguished Masonic philosophers and commentators would agree that this goal is shared with Freemasonry. Indeed, the concepts Plato that imparted through his allegory clearly parallel the teachings of the Craft. It is only natural for an institution defined as "a regular system of morality conceived in a strain of interesting allegory, which readily unfolds its beauties to the candid and industrious enquirer"[24] to be interested in the parallels of those great minds who so effectively used allegories as tools of instruction. We are taught in the second degree to cultivate the Arts and to grow in usefulness. This can be achieved through consistent and serious reflection upon the Craft and its symbols. But Freemasonry is not disconnected from the weave of Western culture, and by exploring useful parallels and searching out those concepts and ideals that closely resemble—and possibly inspired—the teachings of the Craft, we can better understand our philosophical context. May the Order of Freemasonry be as enduring as the teachings of the great philosopher Plato. ⨎

Notes

1   See W. K. C. Guthrie, *A History of Greek Philosophy* (Cambridge, UK: Cambridge University Press, 1979), vol. 4.

2. Debra Nails, *The People of Plato: A Prosopography and Other Socratics* (Indianapolis, Ind.: Hackett, 2002).

3. *Timaeus* 22b.

4. H. Cairns, "Introduction" in *Plato: The Collected Dialogues* (Princeton, N.J.: Princeton University Press, 1961).

5. Manly P. Hall, "Albert Pike: The Plato of Freemasonry," *The Phoenix: An Illustrated Review of Occultism and Philosophy* 1(1931):37–45.

6. Albert Pike, *Morals and Dogma of the Ancient and Accepted Scottish Rite of Freemasonry* (Charleston, S.C.: Supreme Council of the Southern Jurisdiction of the United States, 1871).

7. Pike, *Morals and Dogma*, 617.

8. W. L. Wilmshurst, *The Meaning of Masonry*, Rev. Ed. (San Francisco, Calif.: Plumbstone, 2007), 95.

9. Albert Gallatin Mackey, *The Symbolism of Freemasonry.* Rev. Ed. (San Francisco: Plumbstone, 2011), 27.

10. Hippolyto Joseph da Costa, *A Sketch for the History of the Dionysian Artificers: A Fragment* (London: Sherwood, Neely & Jones, 1820).

11. Plato, *The Republic* 514b–518d. See pp. 72–78 for a translation.

12. T. Z. Lavine, *From Socrates to Sarte: The Philosophic Quest* (New York: Bantam, 1984), 28.

13. Albert Gallatin Mackey, *An Encylopaedia of Freemasonry and its Kindred Sciences* (Philadelphia, Pa.: McClures Publishing Co., 1927), 169.

14. Rex Hutchens, *A Bridge to Light* (Washington, D.C.: Supreme Council of the Ancient and Accepted Scottish Rite of Freemasonry, Southern Jurisdiction, 2000).

15. Pike, *Morals and Dogma*, 3.

16. Ibid., 6.

17. Mackey, *Encylopaedia*, 1007.

18. H. L. Haywood, *The Great Teachings of Masonry* (Kingport, Tenn.: Southern Publishers, 1922).

19. Plato, *The Republic* 515e.

20. Ibid., 516a.

21. Ibid., 516a–b.

22. Lionel Fanthorpe & Patricia Fanthorpe, *Mysteries and Secrets of the Masons: The Story Behind the Masonic Order* (Toronto: Dundurn Press, 2006), 110.

23. Ibid.

24. Definition of Freemasonry from William Preston's original Apprentice degree lecture, as cited in Colin Dyer, *William Preston and His Work* (Shepperton, UK: Lewis Masonic, 1987), 207.

A Song of Degrees: The Aspirant · *W. L. Wilmshurst*

> I will lift up mine eyes to the hills.
>
> Psalms 121:1

I will go up, go up,
　　To the high hill of the Lord;
The world is an empty cup
　　And a Voice in my heart hath stirred
To seek for a long-lost Word.
　　I know of an inward door,
With a guard and a flashing sword,
　　That leads to a chequered floor
And a hall where wise men feast;
　　And my love of the world hath ceased,
I will set my face to the East
　　And sup at their festive board.

And I will go down, go down,
　　Into deep darkling seas
Of knowledge and have renown
　　With those whose business is
In waters of mysteries.
　　Away from the worldly town
And beyond its harbour-bar
　　I will sail where the sun goes down
And steer by a mystic star;

And my stature shall be increased
　　When I go down to the West
And rise with the sun in the East,
　　And so shall my soul have rest.

And I will learn, will learn,
　　Secrets of sky and earth;
As the hart pants I burn
　　For waters of living worth
And a land of godly mirth.
I will cast my clothes at the door
　　Of a house that I need no more,
And I will go hence, go hence,
　　From the arid plains of sense,
And in raiment of innocence
　　I will make my way and rejoice
　　To climb the hill of the Lord
In search of the long-lost Word
　　And the sound of a still small voice.

Thomas Starr King: Apostle of Liberty, Brother of the Craft

Adam G. Kendall

O**N DECEMBER 8, 2009**, nearly one hundred Californians gathered in Sacramento to participate in the rededication of the statue of Thomas Starr King. They were in the state's capitol to welcome the monument home from its seventy-nine year display at the National Statuary Hall in Washington D.C. The seven foot tall bronze of Starr King, sculpted in 1930 by Haig Patigian, was now installed in an outdoor setting: Sacramento's Capital Park. The crowd comprised people from many facets of life, and many of them were linked to Starr King and his legacy. During the ceremony, his descendants, his successors in the Unitarian ministry, and his Masonic brethren all spoke of Starr King's integrity and the lasting impact he made upon the United States. The midday sun cast a golden hew around the statue's features, highlighting majestically the shine of his high forehead and the graceful curve of his fingers upon a regally outstretched right arm, beckoning those assembled to hear his story.

When Thomas Starr King first walked upon California's fertile soil in 1860, just a few months after his thirty-fifth birthday, the new state was dangerously close to either aligning with the Confederate cause in the American Civil War, or seceding to form its own independent republic. He came filled with optimism about his mission, but also an innate sense that his time may have been short. He told a friend in a letter, shortly after sailing into the Golden Gate, "I have passed meridian. It is after twelve o'clock in the large day of my mortal life. I am no longer a young man. It is now afternoon with me, and the shadows turn toward the east."[1]

The young minister was certainly a rare individual. Small of stature and physically weak, his kind eyes, boyish smile, and staggering humility was contradicted by a powerful, booming voice an eloquent prose and an aura of a man who was older and wiser beyond his years. Indeed, his life, as recorded by biographers such as Charles Wendte and William Day Simonds, is almost a lesson in destiny tempered through discipline and integrity: a highly intelligent preacher's son from New

England, he dropped out of school to support his family after the death of his father. While working as a bookkeeper, school teacher and at other jobs, he continued a rigorous self-study in classical literature with the help of his mother, and was eventually called to the pulpit.

According to Simonds, even in his youth Starr King was regarded with deep respect. Henry Parker, who was renowned for his private library and a kind disposition toward those voracious for knowledge, saw latent talents in the young widow's son, and sent him to fill preaching engagements at his direction. Parker once wrote of the young Starr King to a prominent church near Boston, "I cannot come to preach for you as I would like, but with your kind permission I will send Thomas Starr King. This young man is not a regularly ordained preacher, but he has the grace of God in his heart, and the gift of tongues. He is a rare sweet spirit and I know that after you have met with him you will thank me for sending him to you."[2]

His delicate health demanded that he vacation in the countryside, and his time there led to his 1859 book, *The White Hills, Their Legends, Landscape and Poetry*, which solidified his reputation as an early advocate of natural, open spaces in the same vein as his contemporar, Henry David Thoreau. By 1869, Starr King was recognized both by his elders in the Unitarian ministry and the general public on the East Coast as being a gifted writer, preacher, and speaker on par with Ralph Waldo Emerson and Henry Ward Beecher.

By the time he arrived in California from Massachusetts, Starr King's fame preceded him. His views on slavery, nature, and the American Union were strong, and echoed the sentiments of Jefferson, but more particularly those of Elijah Parish Lovejoy, Charles Sumner, John Rogers, and other thinkers of his day.

And so the crowd on this winter day in December of 2009 gathered under the gaze of Starr King's monument to honor the man, who, almost immediately after arriving in San Francisco, turned his attention to preserving California's status in the Union by supporting Lincoln's presidency and utilizing his formidable speaking ability to convince the citizens of the State to consider a united America that would abolish slavery and rejoice in the gifts that Providence had bestowed upon its citizens.

In each of his lectures—on such themes as "Washington," "Lexington and Concord," "Patriotism"—he always made his plea for a united country: "No such soil, so varied by climate, by products, by mineral riches, by forests and lake…no such domain was ever given to one people! What a privilege it is to be an American."[3] From the positive effect his speeches had upon both his supporters and detractors (and the latter were legion), there is little doubt that the claim that he saved California for the Union is true.

Perhaps his message would not have been so effective if he had not bolstered his sentiment with action, for he became well known for supporting those wounded during the Civil War. His passions led him establish the Western chapter of the Sanitation Commission, which promoted and staffed clean hospitals and camps in the Union Army, and to raise 1.2 million dollars— one quarter of the amount accrued for the entire nation—for their benefit. The modern Red Cross is ulimately derived from those efforts.

Starr King's love of nature also caused him to travel extensively throughout California, and to lobby the federal government for the preservation of natural resources so that they might be enjoyed as monuments to the resources from which civilization sprang, for "public use, resort, and recreation."[4] This was almost thirty years before John Muir began his own environmental campaigns. As a result of King's lobbying, 20,000 acres of the Yosemite Valley, which was being hacked away as the result of commercial interests, was designated as protected land by President Lincoln, and after Starr King's death, became the second federally protected park in the United States.

Starr King embodied a potent combination of eloquence and force. He was a humble man that laid bare his opposition's stances by employing honesty, logic and justice. According to Simonds, he argued against his opponents by fairly stating their case, and then, "without unneccesary severity, demolish[ing] it."[5]

His unbending commitment to unity and humanity would lead Starr King to encounter Freemasonry—a fraternity endued with the tradition of bringing together men of different faiths and livelihood under one umbrella of brotherly love, relief and truth. Even before joining the Order, Starr King honored requests to speak on behalf of the Masonic Relief Fund and other Masonic groups.[6] No doubt as a result of connections derived from those speaking engagements, Starr King became a Mason in 1861 in Oriental Lodge № 144 (now Phoenix № 144) in San Francisco, and served as its Chaplain. While his Masonic career was cut short by his untimely death only three years later, even in that short time his oratory skills earned him the appointment of Grand Orator within the recently-formed Grand Lodge of California. In his 1863 oration, he wrote:

The tools of the Craft are representative...of speculative truth and speak to the inward eye of laws and duties that make life and character symmetrical and strong. Yet, though we build no structures such as our ancient brethren reared, though the temples in which we meet are not the monuments of our own proficiency in the art whose instruments we cherish, we are builders and preservers in a richer sense, for our Order itself grows stronger and more precious with years, and its uses are more varied and beautiful with the lapse of time.[7]

Brother Starr King's oration was well received, and in a rare exception to the custom of featuring a different Grand Orator each year, he was asked to remain in the station for a second year, and to prepare another speech for the next annual convention. But his relentless speaking schedule took a toll on his frail body. Driving himself past the point of exhaustion in his work to keep California in the Union, he died on March 4, 1864, of diphtheria at just thirty-nine years of age. He was given a Masonic funeral and buried in San Francisco.[8]

His Masonic brethren have long remembered him as one who truly lived according to the values of the Craft. And so it was fitting that, one hundred forty-five years later, brethren from Starr King's mother lodge and other lodges around California, clad in white aprons, would gather to welcome his statue to Sacramento and bear witness to his memory.

As part of the official program organized by the California State Parks service and the Capitol Museum, Worshipful Brother Gary Allan Peare of Orinda Lodge № 122 addressed the crowd to honor Thomas Starr King's commitment to Freemasonry and humanity:

I am proud to be here today to speak on behalf of the more than sixty thousand Freemasons in California at this public tribute to Thomas Starr King's life as a Patriot, a Californian and as a Freemason. Here with me today are members of several California Masonic Lodges, including Orinda Lodge № 122, of Orinda California,

Academia Lodge № 847 of Oakland, and Phoenix Lodge № 144 of San Francisco, which was the very Lodge Starr King joined when he became a Freemason in 1861.

To Californians, Thomas Starr King was an exemplary citizen who helped mightily in the struggle to preserve the Union in the face of civil war. To Masons, he is remembered as something more: a BROTHER.

In Freemasonry, the young cleric found an expression of primordial wisdom, and an appreciation of its civilizing force. And in Brother Starr King, the Masons of California saw not only eloquence, which was widely known, but more so his truly exemplary devotion to humanity's greater good.

It was not surprising, then, that only a year after he joined our fraternity, he was selected to serve as our Grand Orator. In this position, it was his duty to travel throughout California, speaking at its 170 Lodges, and, ultimately, to address the statewide gathering of Freemasons in 1863.

In his historic oration on that occasion, Brother Starr King said, "the Order of Masonry, the quiet efficiency of its organism, the regard for forms it fosters, the love of order it induces and deepens, the graceful habits of submission it educates, and the sacredness it pours around organic law and the seats of authority."

"All these," he said, "are a prominent portion of the bonds of civilization in our country." This is, precisely, the way in which Freemasonry has endeavored to reinforce the commitment to civility in our society. The re-cultivation of this quality within the domain of our public discourse—the rekindling of *true civil discourse*—is a need keenly felt today, as we see daily examples of how polarized our consideration of today's great issues has become.

Brother Starr King, your memorial statue stands as a towering reminder to us of our universal, solemn, and personal duty to become "builders in a richer sense." To find that center of union that can enable us to see past our prejudices and beyond our legitimate differences of opinion, so we may learn from, and better understand, those who might otherwise have remained at a perpetual distance. This virtue—this very virtue—remains one of the key lessons we are taught as Freemasons.[9]

After these final remarks, the ceremony concluded, and those present attended a special exhibit inside the Capitol building, featuring a few possessions of Starr King. I wondered what he had been thinking the last time he touched these. What was going through his mind? Was there self-doubt? Was there fear? Was there a quiet surplus of faith and strength? All of these things were within this small man, barely 5′4″, but his lion's roar of a voice tempered with the melodious words as if from a harp, would make the world listen—if just for a moment—and to see themselves within the eyes of their neighbor. ⨏

Notes

Special thanks to Koren Benoit, Curator at the California State Senate, and to the staff of the California Department of Parks and Recreation for their valuable assistance in making arrangements for Masonic participation in the rededication ceremony.

1. Letter to Randolph Ryder, 17 December, 1860. Reprinted in Richard Frothingham, *A Tribute to Thomas Starr King* (Boston: Ticknor & Fields, 1865), 196.

2. William Day Simonds, *Starr King in California* (San Francisco: Paul Elder & Co., 1917), 5–6.

3. Thomas Starr King, *Substance and Show, and Other Lectures.* Eighth Edition. (Boston: Houghton, Mifflin & Co., 1890), 397.

M∴W∴ Bro∴ Ellsworth Meyer, then Grand Master of Masons in California, addresses the gathering at the dedication of the Starr King Memorial at the First Unitarian Church in San Francisco, October 8, 1950. Seated, from left to right, are Boswell F. King, Jr., Boswell F. King, Sr., John B. McGovern, Admiral U.S.N. (Ret.), Starr Warner, Mrs. Margery Davis Warner, Mrs. Boswell F. King, Jr. Mrs. Boswell F. King, Sr., Mrs. Norris K. Davis, Norris K. Davis. In the words of Grand Master Meyer, "It has been said that to live in the hearts of those we leave behind, is not to die. Of Thomas Starr King, we say: He yet lives in the hearts of Californians, he yet lives in the hearts of Masons." Image courtesy the Henry Wilson Coil Library and Museum of Freemasonry, San Franicisco, California.

4. Peter J. Blodgett, "Visiting the 'Realm of Wonder': Yosemite and the Business of Tourism, 1855–1916." In Richard J. Orsi, Alfred Runte, Marlene Smith-Baranzini, Eds., *Yosemite and Sequoia: A Century of California National Parks* (Berkeley: University of California Press, 1993), 34.

5. Simonds, *Starr King in California*, 47.

6. Frothingham, *Tribute to Thomas Starr King*, 181.

7. Thomas Starr King, Grand Oration (Grand Lodge of California Proceedings, 1863), 113–17; see the full text under the feature, "Our Conscious Temple," pp. 94–101.

8. Starr King's Masonic funeral was conducted under the direction of Alfred B. Kittredge. See Frothingham, *Tribute to Thomas Starr King*, 227.

9. The oration was coauthored by Shawn Eyer of Academia Lodge № 847 and Gary Allan Peare of Orinda Lodge № 122.

Our Conscious Temple

Thomas Starr King

GRAND ORATOR, 1863–1864
GRAND LODGE OF FREE & ACCEPTED MASONS OF CALIFORNIA

MOST WORSHIPFUL GRAND MASTER AND BRETHREN OF THE GRAND LODGE: In offering salutation to you, with cordial thanks for the honor and privilege connected with the office and duty which you have entrusted to me, I shall only attempt briefly, in the discharge of that duty, to note two or three points of harmony and correspondence between the structure and working of our Order, and the handiwork of the Almighty in the external world.

We belong to the great Fraternity of Free and Accepted Masons. The implements of our Craft, however, are no longer for operative toil. We do not now, as part of our covenant, set fast the Doric pillar, nor release from marble the ornament of the Corinthian capital. We no longer sketch the complications of Gothic piles, and cement the buttresses of haughty towers, and carry up, course by course, the aspiring stones of pinnacles. The tools of the Craft are representative now of specnlative truth, and speak to the inward eye of laws and duties that make life nobie and character symmetrical and strong. Yet, though we build no structures such as our ancient brethren reared, though the temples in which we meet are not the monuments of our own proficiency in the art whose instruments we cherish, we are builders and preservers in a richer sense; for our Order itself grows stronger and more precious with years, and its uses are more varied and beautiful with the lapse of time.

The Masonic organization is far more remarkable and wonderful than the noblest edifice it ever added to the landscape of history. Let us pause, brethren, on the word "organization." That is the great word of the world. The Almighty is *the Organizer*. He creates elements in order to mingle and fraternize them in composition and products. In the original chaos matter was unorganized. The process of is death is dis–organization. All the marvels of beauty, all the victories of life, are exhibitions and triumphs of organizing force. The most fascinating chapters of science are those which unveil to us the vast fields which the forces traverse that sustain highest forms of life upon the globe.

A crystallized gem is the most attractive form of solid matter, because more thought and skill are expended in its structure than in any other stony combination of atoms. A flower is of a higher order of charm, for more various and more subtle elements are wrought into its composite loveliness; and then the provisions for the growth and support of the flower affect us more profoundly still — the mixture of the air, the various powers hidden in the sun-ray, the alternation of daylight

and gloom, the laws of evaporation and of clouds, and the currents in the air that carry moisture from zone to zone for the nutriment of vegetation. We soon find in nature that no element, or force, exists unrelated. It is in harness with other elements for a common labor, and an interchange of service for a common end. *Organization* is the idea

> HOW OFTEN we read, or hear with pride, that in the building of the first temple . . . there was neither hammer, nor ax, nor any tool of iron heard in the house while it was building! What is that to the growth of our Order itself? How quiet the process, yet how constant! Who hears the noise of it?

which science impresses upon us as the secret of life, health, power and beauty in her realm. An organized product can appear only from forces of nature, which are the movements of the Divine will. Man can arrange, manufacture, weave, forge, adjust, refine; but he cannot organize as nature does. He can make machines through which the forces of nature will play for cunning ends; cannot conjure the principle of life into any mould of his making. He can start shuttles that will weave a carpet for the reception room of a palace in one loom; but he can build no mill, he can start no laboratory, where the warp and woof of the banana leaf can be plaited. He can tell how the sugar is secreted in the veins of a clover blossom; but

he cannot make the clover seed. And yon might as well ask the wisest scientific man to fashion a world, as to create one of the green needles which a pine tree produces by the million, or one of the innumerable blades of grass.

But the great glory of organization is when it is revealed in human life. The highest structure of the creative art is the body of man, representing in its complexity and the friendly partnership of its powers, the system and co-ordination which society should attain; and it is a marked epoch in history when a new movement is made which succeeds in organizing men widely and permanently for noble and beneficent ends.

We are not intended to be separate, private persons, but rather fibres, fingers, and limbs. The aim of religion is not to perfect us as persons, looking at each of us apart from others. The Creator does not propose to polish souls like so many pins — each one dropping off clean and shiny, with no more organic relations to each other than pins have on a card. We are made to be rather like the steel, the iron, and the brass, which are compacted into an engine, where no modest bolt or rivet is placed so that it does not somehow contribute to the motion, or increase the efficiency of the organism.

In savage life men are slightly organized. A savage tribe is like a heap of sand; the atoms are distinct; they are aggregated, not combined; no beautiful product springs from them; and the first wind of disaster blows them away. A half-civilized nation is but slightly organized, so far as noble purposes and high sentiments are concerned. Progress is marked by wider, higher, finer developments, issuing from the combination and co-partnership of souls. There can be no such thing as justice, until men, in large masses, are rightly related to each other. There can be no prosperity in a community until the majority of its people are so organized that their minds receive training, and their energies are unfettered. There can be no happiness, except as the result of proper relations permanently established between the different classes or strata of the social world.

"No man liveth to himself." "Whether one member suffer, all the members suffer or one member be honored, all the members rejoice with it." "How good and how pleasant it is for brethren to dwell together in unity!" When a compacted unity of living beings is seen, one of the most precious objects for which the world was built is attained. A large and well-ordered family is such a jewel. A neighborhood at peace, and free from scandal, is — or, rather I should say, *would* be — a still more precious jewel of the same quality. A state, a nation, so constructed that the forces of all ranks of its inhabitants should be brought into play, and the rights of all ranks should be saved from pressure, would be a more marvelous and a more inspiring structure than the material order and harmony of our solid globe.

It is in the light of this principle that the value and nobleness of *Masonry* appear. I say again that no edifice which our ancient brethren reared was equal to the living structure of which they and we are portions. How often we read, or hear with pride, that in the building of the first temple, the stones were made ready before they were brought together; so that there was neither hammer, nor ax, nor any tool of iron heard in the house while it was building! What is that to the growth of our Order itself? How quiet the process, yet how constant! Who hears the noise of it? Who sees, or knows, when the sound timber and the approved stones are brought together, and fitted, and lifted to their place amidst the roar, and strife, and selfishness of the world? Yet, in thousands of towns and cities of the world, in all its zones, in almost all communities and tongues of men, this work, in substantial sameness of method and pledge, is going on. The Temple of Solomon

must stand as it was built. It could not enlarge itself. It could not bud with smaller temples, and then take them in under a widening roof or a swelling dome. Neither, when some of its pillars decayed, could it restore its own decrease, as the living cedars of Lebanon repair their wastes and renew their leaves. But our conscious temple does all this, and noiselessly. It fills in its losses; it enlarges its sweep and sway; it does it through men of all conditions, and classes, and races; and still it stands in its old proportions, though in greater amplitude, symmetrical, mysterious, and sublime.

This is the most remarkable social organization of the world. None on the globe, with half so many elements in its composition, is so old. We are told of late that excavations made under modern Jerusalem disclose remnants of the old city in various periods of its history. Portions of the massive masonry of the time of Solomon are uncovered. Above these appear fragments of the work of Zerubbabel. On a higher historic stratum are specimens of workmanship from the age of Herod the Great; and still above these, but below the level of the present city, are remains of the constructive toil ordered by Justinian. We delight to feel, brethren, that the past, measured by as many ages, is under us; but it is not beneath us in a broken symmetry, and a dead grandeur, as under Jerusalem. It is rather beneath us as the roots are beneath a tree, and as the central rings are hidden in the trunk. They give power and pith to the structure still. They are part of its present majesty, sources of its living vigor, prophecies of its future strength.

We should take satisfaction, brethren, nay, a noble pride, in the consciousness of the age and vastness of our organization. If a stone in St. Peters' could be conscious, or any portion of the wall, or spire, of Strasburg Cathedral, do you not think that it would rejoice in its position, that it would be exultant over its partnership with other stones in rearing the grandeur of such a pile for such worthy uses? If any fragment of such an edifice could be conscious, and did not feel any pride, or any privilege, in its position and its call, would its indifference be a merit, or a shame rather? How shall it be with us? Shall we not feel that there is dignity, that there is privilege, in being living fibres of an organization which has passed from one era of the world to another, which is older than the oldest empire of Christendom, which has on its rail names that sparkle in history like the sovereign stars, and which exists, not for purposes of private aggrandizement, or the selfish joy of its members, but to give deeper root to good principles in the world, and to diffuse the spirit of peace and order? If a Mason is not grateful and glad over his fellowship, it is because he does not appreciate the value in the world of the organization of good.

The idea of organization is connected with the idea of *order*. And here, also, Masonry reflects to us, or rather illustrates in a higher form, the wisdom breathed by the Great Architect through nature. It is said that order is heaven's first law. It is no less true, brethren, that it is earth's first privilege. It is the condition of beauty of liberty, and of peace.

Think how the principle of order for all the orbs of the solar system is hidden in the sun. The tremendous power of his gravitation reaches thousands of millions of miles, and hampers the self-will — the centrifugal force — of mighty Jupiter, of Uranus with his staff of moons, of cold, and distant, and invisible Neptune. *There's* a Grand Lodge for you, in which these separate Masters are held in check by the Most Worshipful Grand Master's power! Nay, they tell us now of a central sun around which all other suns, those fixed stars of the firmament, bend and sweep. If this suggests an argument by analogy in favor of a world congress of Masons, with a Grand Lodge of Nations, and a Supreme Master, whose power runs over seas and across continents, girdling the earth like a magnetic stream, I leave it to be discussed by the Committee on Correspondence, in the next volume of our Grand Secretary's admirable reports. But, in the case of our planetary system, is it any hardship that the separate globes are so strictly under rule, and pay obeisance to the sun? Is it not their chief blessing, their sovereign privilege? What if the order were less strict and punctual; what if the force in these globes, that chafes under the central rein and champs its curb, should be triumphant for a day? What if the earth should gain liberty against the pull of the sun? Beauty from that moment would begin to wither fertility would begin to shrivel. The hour of seeming freedom would be the dawn of anarchy; for the sun's role and apparent despotism is only the stern and beneficent condition of perpetual harmony, bounty, and joy.

Everywhere, order is the great interest. What humanity needs is the fulfillment of these indications of nature, freedom with order, a proper consciousness of worth in every breast, a recognition by each man of the worth and claims of every other, and an acknowledgment by all of a common and controlling law. This idea of order fulfilled in the architecture of nature, is committed as a trust to our Fraternity and the proper reverence for it is poured out continually through the influence of our hallowed bonds.

For every country that influence is silently wholesome. In lands where the spirit of society does not recognize sufficiently the worth of man, but pays too much homage to rank and name, our Order quietly fosters the principle of the equality of privilege and responsibility under the laws of everlasting justice; and, without being revolutionary, it upholds the honor of human nature, and patiently rebukes despotic arrogance and

> The chief difference between a very wise man…and an ignorant one is, not that the first is acquainted with regions invisible to the second, away from common sight and interest, but that he understands the common things which the second only sees.
>
> —Bro∴ Thomas Starr King

aristocratic scorn. In our own country its service is of a different kind. We need more respect for authority, less self-will, a deeper sense of the sacredness of law, and education in the habits, manners, and feeling of deference and loyalty. The rupture of our National Unity, for a time, with its tremendous costs in treasure, blood, and agony, is in part the revelation, in part the penalty, in part, perhaps, through the severe beneficence of God, the cure of our chronic insubordination of character to the authority and sanctity of high principles, which has unfitted us, all over the land, to handle the sacred responsibilities and delicate trusts of imperial statesmanship and continental government. Whatever will teach our people reverence, decorum, respect for others in the utterance and defense of opinion, submission to constituted authority with dignity and grace, will be medicine for our trouble, and will prepare for us a better future. I believe that the Order of Masonry, the quiet efficiency of its organism, the

regard for forms it fosters, the love of order it induces and deepens, the graceful habits of submission it educates, and the sacredness it pours around organic law and the seats of authority, are a prominent portion of the bonds of civilization in our country, and an immense blessing when we consider our natural perils.

Brethren, let us cherish the duties and trusts of our Fraternity for this good influence that it so naturally and liberally expends. Let us resolve, as part of our duty to the Creator, the source of order and law, to drink more deeply of the springs, within our enclosure, whose issue is healing and reviving. In the maintenance of the bond and customs of order is the pledge of our prosperity, as well as the assurance of our service. *Order has limits.* Let us continue to guard sacredly our limits, to suffer no transgression of them. What a power is represented in the men who have gathered within this temple, during the present week, to superintend our general interests and interpret and apply our law! What harmony has prevailed here, what decorum of speech, what promptness in duty, what efficiency in protecting and guarding the common good! A visitor from outside our fellowship, suddenly brought in here to look, for a moment, at the representative men thus gathered from all sections of our State domain, and to observe, by one glance, the quiet power embodied in the assembly, might imagine, if suddenly taken out again, that there could be something perilous to the public welfare in the association, by secret ties, of so many men of such varied ability, working in seclusion from public criticism and without passion. He would feel secure again by knowing that it is only by keeping rigidly to the work of fostering the interests of the Order, that the dignity, the calm, the freedom from passion, the efficiency, are manifest or possible. Let any other question be intruded here, and there could be no detriment to public interests; for our harmony would break. Volcanic flame and blackness would burst through the lofty and snowy peace. By keeping within our limits alone are we prosperous and orderly; and within our limits our prosperity is the welfare of the community, the good of the State, the strengthening of civilization. Rejoice, brethren, in your privilege; wall off from intrusion the garden of order you have received; and guard the book of your Constitution with the Tyler's sword.

Organization and Order! In preserving these we are in harmony with the will and work of the Sovereign Architect, published in the harmony, dignity, and peace of nature. And one other word must be spoken, so familiar, so precious, to the Masonic ear and heart. You anticipate what it is — *Charity*. In nature, which speaks the wisdom and character of the Invisible Spirit, organization is not for the sate of wisdom and skill chiefly — order is not for the sake of law and obedience chiefly — but all for the sake of *Charity*. There is harmony and stability that there may be breadth of bounty, constancy in giving wherever there is need. Within every district of nature there is beneficence to all the need within that district, and then a pouring out of alms into a general fund of bounty and cheer.

Every mountain upholds and supports the herbage on its slopes, and sends off rills to carry down soil to the vales and plains, while they feed herbage there. You cannot find a tree, or plant, or flower, that lives for itself. The animal world breathes out gases for the vegetable kingdom, and then the vegetable world exhales or stores up some elements essential to animal health and vigor. The carbonic acid we breathe out here and which is poison to us, blown eastward by our west winds, may be greedily taken up, a few days hence, by vineyards on the slopes of the Sierra, and returned to us in the sweetness of the grape. The equator "sends greeting" to the Arctic zone by the warm gulf stream that flows near the polar coasts to soften their winds. The poles return a colder stream and add an embassy of icebergs, too, to temper the fierce tropic heats. Selfishness is condemned by the still harmonies of the creation. Perfect order issues out of interwoven service.

Do we ever get tired of the toils and tax of charity? Suppose the sun did. What does it receive in homage or obedience from the orbs that swing round him, in comparison with what he gives—all his light, all his heat, all his vitality for the blessing of four score worlds! Shall we complain of the demand upon our treasuries, or our private purses, for the sacred funds of the Masonic Board of Belief? What if the sea grumbled at the assessment which the mighty gun — the Most Worshipful Grand Master of the system — levies on his substance? Every day the sun touches its stores with its wand of light and says *give, give*. And it obeys. Evaporation is its tax constantly demanded, constantly given. Remember, brethren, that every cloud you see, whether stretched in a beautiful bar across the east at sunrise, or hanging in pomp over the gorgeous pavilion of the retiring day, is part of the contribution for the general relief of nature assessed by the lordly sun. The water which the ocean *keeps* is salt. Pour a bucket of it on a hill of corn, or a garden bed, and it kills it. The water which the ocean gives is fresh, and descends in blessing, after it rides in beauty or majesty on the viewless couriers of the air. Nature tells us that "to give is to live."

Society is struggling up to reach the order which nature thus indicates. Civilization is yet in its infancy. There is no town, no village, of Christendom yet where the bounty of nature to all the needy is fulfilled. Let us be grateful, brethren, that, within our fellowship, charity is organized, as well as law and peace. Our treasury has no avarice in it. The oil poured upon our head flows to the end of the beard and the garment's hem.

How good and how precious it is for brethren to dwell in such unity! May it continue, brothers, and widen through our fidelity and service and beneficence! God preserve our organization, guard our Order, inspire our beneficence, and grant that, a century hence, our successors may meet here to enjoy in a larger fellowship the result of our faithfulness, and within a nation not sundered, but presided over by one Grand Master, heir of the virtues, the hope, and the blessing of WASHINGTON! ✝

On motion of Bro. William H. Hill, it was —
Resolved, That the thanks of the Grand Lodge be tendered to the Grand Orator for the beautiful address just delivered by him; and that a copy thereof be requested for publication with the proceedings of this Communication.

Oration delivered by Thomas Starr King on May 16, 1863 in San Francisco, California. Reprinted from the 1863 Proceedings of the Grand Lodge of California, pp. 112–17.

Silence and Solemnity in Craft Freemasonry

Shawn Eyer

סיג לחכמה שתיקה.
Silence is Wisdom's security fence.

Rabbi Akiva

Cease Clamour and Faction,
 Oh, cease,
Fly hence all ye cynical train;
Disturb not, disturb not the Lodge's
 sweet peace,
Where Silence and Secrecy reign.

The Freemasons' Ode, 1781

T HE PROFOUND SILENCE of a tiled Lodge during ceremonies such as the initiation of a candidate can be deeply impressive, and naturally induces solemn reflections upon the essential meaning of the work. Pythagoras taught that a man should "either remain silent, or say something better than the silence he disturbs."[1] This is certainly consistent with Masonic practice, for within a tiled lodge, brethren are expected not to converse in a casual way, as if the lodge were no different from the street outside.

It is often pointed out that early British and American Freemasons had no lodge buildings of their own, but met in rented rooms available above the taverns of that period. This has sometimes given rise to a misconception that their lodge meetings were only boisterous social affairs, devoid of solemnity. In fact, it is often stated that Freemasonry "began" in taverns. Not only is this untrue, but it is often taken as evidence that the early Craft had no serious philosophical concerns, that the rituals were little more than a game designed to entertain inebriated gentlemen, and that the idea of taking Freemasonry seriously as a contemplative and philosophical tradition was introduced at a much later date. But an examination of early records presents many challenges to such a view, and allows us to see beyond the toasts and songs of the festive boards to understand other elements of the culture of the lodges of centuries past.

Prescriptions of Silence in Early Freemasonry

In Scotland, where many believe speculative Freemasonry was born, the lodges did *not* meet in taverns, but in private buildings or the out-of-doors. For example, see the regulation that is recorded in the "Lawes and Statutes Ordained be the Honourable Lodge Aberdein," adopted on the Feast of St. John the Evangelist, December 27, 1670:

> Wee ordaine lykwayes that no Lodge be holden within a dwelling house where there is people living in it, but in the open fields except it be ill weather, and then let there be a house chosen that no person shall heir nor sie us.[2]

The same 1670 bylaws emphasize that there is to be no side-chatter in a lodge while it is meeting—even whispering is forbidden:

> Wee ordaine lykwayes that none of our number shall whisper or round together [whisper together] in company with us without leave asked and given, all under the faylzie [penalty] of the law of the Lodge or the will of the company.[3]

These regulations show a Craft highly concerned with both the preservation of its secrets (including, apparently, gestures as well as words) and with the maintenance of a solemn order within the lodge while it was in session.

The lodge at Aberdeen's influence should not be taken lightly, for it is distinguished in a number of ways. A notable example is that the first known speculative Masons to immigrate to the New World were from that very lodge.[4]

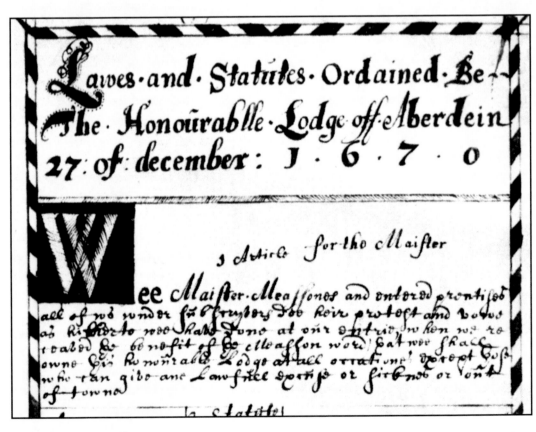

Lawes·and·Statutes·Ordained·Be·
The·Honourablle·Lodge·off·Aberdein
27·of·december: J·6·7·0

More importantly, the Secretary of the Aberdeen Lodge was a glassmaker named James Anderson—the father of the more familiar Rev. James Anderson (1678–1739). The "Lawes and Statutes" book that still survives is actually in the senior Bro∴ Anderson's handwriting.[5]

After the first Grand Lodge of England was founded in 1717 in London, Rev. James Anderson was selected to produce its first book of constitutions. The junior Anderson was most likely initiated in his father's Aberdeen lodge, and as such would have been familiar with its rules on maintaining due solemnity.[6]

Echoing the Aberdeen statutes, the 1723 first edition of Anderson's *Constitutions* stressed the seriousness of the ritualistic work and the importance of remaining completely silent while the lodge is opened unless one is recognized from the Chair:

> You are not to hold private Committees, or separate Conversation, without Leave from the Master, nor to talk of any thing impertinent or unseemly, nor interrupt the Master or Wardens, or any Brother speaking to the Master: Nor behave yourself ludicrously or jestingly while the Lodge is engaged in what is serious and solemn; nor use any unbecoming Language upon any Pretence whatsoever; but to pay due Reverence to your Master, Wardens, and Fellows, and put them to worship.[7]

When the Antients published their own book of constitutions in 1756, the same strict emphasis on decorum was included.[8] The above-cited

◀ The first page of the 1670 laws and statutes of Aberdeen Lodge. The calligraphy is in the hand of James Anderson. He was the lodge's Secretary and Past Master, and the father of Rev. James Anderson, who wrote the first book of Constitutions for the London Grand Lodge in 1723.

regulations, from before and after the beginning of the Grand Lodge era, should not be interpreted to mean that the early Masons did not drink, laugh, sing and celebrate—we know that they did so in abundance while at refreshment. But if it was ever widely acceptable to perform initiations during a lodge's period of refreshment, or to talk, laugh, eat and drink freely while an initiation was taking place, this is neither reflected in nor easily squared with the official regulations of either the Antients or the Moderns.[9] Nor do the various major exposés of the Craft suggest a rowdy intemperance during the actual rituals—an accusation that would have been prominent had such conditions been either universal or widespread.[10]

A generation after the 1723 *Constitutions*, there is some evidence that is suggestive of a single toast being given during the Apprentice degree, where (after the obligation is completed) the Master offers a health "to the Heart that conceals, and to the Tongue that never reveals." According to one source, this toast was called the *Funde Merum Genio*, the "libation to the spirit."[11] But upon closer examination, it appears that this was not done during the initiation itself, but in the course of the catechetical lecture of the first degree, which was given—after the actual initiation—at the banquet table.[12]

By 1769, some brethren even began to criticize the common practice of English and American lodges to meet above taverns in the name of maintaining a solemn image and demeanor. Observing that Scottish and European lodges met in buildings dedicated to Freemasonry alone, James Galloway reached the conclusion that "our meeting at the houses of publicans gives us the air of a *Bacchanalian* society, instead of that appearance of *gravity* and *wisdom* which our order *justly* requires."[13] Sentiments like those expressed in Galloway's letter actually culminated, in 1776, in the erection of London's first Freemason's Hall, near the present location of the headquarters of United Grand Lodge of England.

The above examples from the seventeeth and eighteenth centuries delineate a strong, mainstream tendency among many early Freemasons to cultivate and protect the solemnity of the lodge experience. Surely not all lodges were silent and serious during their labors—but some of them must have been, if they worked in a manner consistent with the regulations put forward by the Grand Lodges of both the Antients and the Moderns.

Solemn Atmosphere, Silent Sanctuary

The purposes of the traditional silence are open to many interpretations. It may have begun simply as a way to maintain order and due respect. But by the latter half of the seventeenth century, as seen (for example) in Galloway's statement, Freemasons were already associating the "serious and solemn" atmosphere of the lodge that Anderson wrote about in 1723 with the profundity of the Masonic teachings.

Certainly, depending upon the setting and current cultural trends, the level of formality and decorum in lodges has varied. In some cases, a more or less casual observance has enjoyed a period of popularity. However, many Freemasons have recently been exploring the benefits of returning to the traditional model of lodge decorum as defined by Anderson and many others through the centuries.

Lodges that stress the preservation of solemnity and dignity do so in order to maintain a serious atmosphere that they see as appropriate to the performance of Masonic ceremonies, especially the conferral of degrees. The overall effect of such a respectful approach to the work is beautifully described by the Masonic philosopher W. L. Wilmshurst, who taught that an ideal Lodge, when properly tiled and duly opened,

> would be a sanctuary of silence and contemplation, broken only by ceremonial utterances or such words of competent and luminous instruction as the Master or Past Masters are moved to extend. And the higher the degree in which it is opened, the deeper and more solemn would be the sense of excluding all temporal thoughts and interests and of approaching more nearly that veiled central Light whose opening into activity in our hearts we profess to be our predominant wish. In such circumstances each Lodge meeting would become an occasion of profound spiritual experience. No member would wish to disturb the harmony of such a Lodge by talk or alien thought.[14]

So important is a deep and abiding silence to the dignity of the degree conferrals that Masons have often introduced symbolic images and slogans to remind one another of the requirement never to disturb the solemnity of the lodge while at labor. Several of these will be explored in the sections to follow.

A Goddess of Silence

The Craft has traditionally personified this important characteristic of a properly opened Lodge as an *allegorical figure*. Such figures, intended to represent "a moral quality or larger concept" in human form,[15] are common in Freemasonry: the best-known today being Faith, Hope, Charity, Temperance, Fortitude, Prudence and Justice. The American work retains Father Time and a weeping virgin, the latter being a personification of the unfinished Temple.

An allegorical figure may be present either through an overt architectural feature such as a statue, or by means of a literary allusion—or, in the case of speculative Freemasonry, a ritualistic reference.

One early literary example, John Bancks' *To Masonry: An Ode* (circa 1730), entreats: "Come...Silence, Guardian of the Door!"[16] The allegorical figure of Silence was frequently referenced in the forms of ancient gods named Harpocrates and Angerona, both of whom are typically shown holding a finger to their lips.

Although Harpocrates seems more familiar to Masons today, actually Angerona was traditionally the more popular of the two. She was a deity in the Roman pantheon, considered to be the goddess of secrecy. She was also known as Diva Angerona and Ancharia, and may have been identical with or conceptually linked to Volupia, the goddess of pleasure.[17] Her most important duty was the maintenance of perfect secrecy. December 21 marked the Divalia or Angeronalia, her annual festival, which was held in the temple of Volupia. The priests gathered there to offer sacrifices before her statue. This image depicted Angerona with her finger held up over her mouth, which was itself bound and sealed. The ancient Roman writer Pliny the Elder (23–79 CE) says that this ceremony "bears especial reference to the inculcation of silence on religious matters."[18] One of the secrets she guarded was the secret or mystical name of Rome, "long kept buried in secrecy with the strictest fidelity and in respectful and salutary silence,"[19] the divulgence of which would imperil the city. Her name means "she who raises up," and this may refer to the finger raised to

her lips, her role of guarding the city, or her connection to the rebirth of the sun—or any combination of the three.

Angerona is perhaps first mentioned by name Masonically in 1756 by Lawrence Dermott in his *Ahiman Rezon*: "The Romans had a Goddess of Silence named Angerona, which was pictured like Harpocrates, holding her Finger on her Mouth, in Token of Secrecy."[20] Some later monitors add: "Hence the Latin sentence *linguam digito compesce*, check your tongue by your finger."[21]

Angerona is also described in similar terms by a number of key writers belonging to the Moderns, such as Wellins Calcott, William Hutchinson and William Preston.[22]

Her characteristic gesture was referenced not only in Masonic literature, but in artwork. An elaborate allegorical engraving of 1755 (see page 85) depicts a Freemason making the sign of silence, while above him a cherub bearing

▶ The figure of Silence, depicted guarding the altar within a lodge room, from the title page of *The Free-Masons' Calendar*, published in London in 1775.

a banner with the motto "Silence and Secrecy" does the same.[23]

An early Masonic image of Angerona is plainly visible on the frontispiece of the *Free-Mason's Calendar and Almanac* of 1775. Although the drawing is poorly executed, it says much. The goddess holds close to the altar in the center of the Lodge, her fingers to her lips. Above the drawing is the motto *Est et fideli tuta silentio merces*, a saying from the Latin poet Horace. This translates, "There is, indeed, a sure reward for trusty silence."[24]

Lodges named for Angerona have existed in Arkansas, Missouri, New York, Pennsylvania, and Tennessee; Eastern Star chapters have also been named after her. Mackey's *Encyclopædia* reports that "her statue has sometimes been introduced among the ornaments of Masonic edifices."[25] Corroborating this, we know that prominent sculptures of a goddess of Silence were commissioned for several important Masonic temples, including the Grand Lodges of Pennsylvania[26] and New York,[27] and the Scottish Rite Temple of Guthrie, Oklahoma. They were not mere decorations, but were all—at least originally—placed so that brethren would pass by them on their way into tiled spaces, reminding each Freemason of his obligations to observe proper decorum.

Angerona or Silence even made her appearance in Masonic ritual at one time. Colin Dyer, a prominent twentieth-century scholar of the development of Masonic ritual, identified a "system of Masonic working from before 1760 right up to the time of the [1813] Union" that survives in several books and manuscript sources.[28] In the manuscripts, one of which dates at least to 1773, the personification of Silence plays a direct role:

> *Now Brother, your Lodge thus built, cemented, ornamented, furnished and dedicated, how is the door secured?*
> Silence locks the door, and deposits the Key.
>
> *Where is the Key deposited?*
> In every true, just and honest Mason's heart.
>
> *Now Brother, after it has been thus finished and locked up, how does it stand?*
> As every honest Mason stands, upright on the Square, fronting the four cardinal points of Heaven with extended arms, ready to receive and comfort the worthy and deserving from all four points.

▲ First Seal of the Antient Grand Lodge of England, founded in 1751, depicting the traditional "wavy" or flaming sword of the Tiler guarding the interlaced Square and Compasses.

▶ Allegorical statue of Silence by William Rush, the first great sculptor of the early American Republic, as displayed at the gothic-style temple of the Grand Lodge of Pennsylvania in Philadelphia. It was commissioned in 1820 by the Grand Lodge, which resolved "that a figure of Silence be placed in the niche on the Stairs." The wooden figure, crafted in 1821, holds a small flame of illumination in her left hand; this torch is actually fitted with piping for use as a gaslight. Photography by Thomas J. Monteforte.

When Silence shut the door of your Lodge, what charge did she give you?

She required me to do Justly, love Mercy, to walk humbly with my God, and to remember my three duties that I might be a welcome guest whenever I returned.[29]

A Silent Lecture

The expression found in the above lecture that the Freemason "stands, upright on the Square, fronting the four cardinal points of Heaven with extended arms" is particularly fascinating, because ritualistic parallels to it exist. Another sign associated with Silence, the ancient "sign of Harpocrates," has also sometimes been used as a Masonic gesture—sometimes even at public ceremonies. In one example, the April 16, 1841 cornerstone-laying of a new Masonic hall for the brethren of the city of Lincoln in England, we see an intriguing nonverbal lesson enacted before some two hundred guests, including the venerable interpreter of Masonic philosophy George Oliver and novelist Edward George Bulwer-Lytton:

> [. . . The] architect [of the hall] . . . produced the plans for the inspection of the Prov. Grand Master. The D[eptuy] P[rovincial] G[rand] M[aster] turning to the Master of the Lodge, said, "Worshipful Master, what will your Lodge be like?" To this no answer was given, but the W. Master pointed up to the heavens, then down to the earth, and then extended his hands horizontally, pointing outwards. The D.P.G.M. then said, "That is a good plan, W.M., but what more have you to

◀ W∴ Bro∴ Gary Peare demonstrates the "silent lecture" found in the January, 1842 issue of *Freemason's Monthly Magazine*. Photography by W∴ Bro∴ Dick Hixson.

tell me?" No answer was made, but the Master first placed his right hand upon his heart, and afterwards his left to his lips. The D.P.G.M. said, "The Master does well, Brothers; let us copy his example," on which each member gave the same signal of sincerity and silence.[30]

This extremely evocative ceremony powerfully recalls the duty of every Master to ensure that his Lodge continually strives toward the emulation of the ideal which is symbolized by the Masonic notion of the Celestial Lodge. As he "stands, upright on the Square, fronting the four cardinal points of Heaven with extended arms," he makes it clear that the purpose of this connection between the upper and lower realms has in mind the benefit of the wider community as well as the inner lives of its brethren ("ready to receive and comfort the worthy and deserving from all four points"). And finally, when he goes on the sign of fidelity and silence, he vows to maintain his Masonic loyalties intact, and to preserve the mysteries inviolate.

There is something of a parallel found between the symbolic gestures above and a certain ritual of the Masonic Rosicrucians, dating back to the 1867 formation of the Societas Rosicruciana in London; intriguingly, Lord Bulwer-Lytton—who was present at the "silent lecture" in Lincoln in 1841—was nominally involved with the Societas Rosicruciana for a brief period as its Grand Patron.[31]

Silence & Circumspection

Just as the ideal of Masonic silence can be personified in the allegorical figures of Harpocrates and Angerona, so it is intended to be realized in the life of every initiate. It is no mere abstract, but is intended to be an essential part of our applied Masonry—practiced even when we are not in Lodge. Indeed, William Preston taught that silence is "the Mason's chief virtue,"[32] and that "[of] all the arts which the Masons profess, the art of secrecy particularly distinguishes them. Taciturnity is a proof of wisdom, and is of the utmost importance in the different transactions of life."[33] Similarly, in most forms of the American work, the Monitor instructs us that:

> The Book of Constitutions, Guarded by the Tyler's Sword, reminds us that we should be ever watchful and guarded in our thoughts, words and actions, particularly when before the uninitiated; ever bearing in remembrance those truly Masonic virtues, silence and circumspection.[34]

Such virtues are internal traits, most effectively cultivated through careful self-reflection. The annual Installation Ritual makes it explicit that the Tiler's sword is something that, in a way, we all carry:

> As the sword is placed in the hands of the Tyler, to enable him effectually to guard against the approach of cowans and eavesdroppers, and suffer none to pass or repass except those who are duly qualified, so it should admonish us to set a guard over our thoughts, a watch at our lips, post a sentinel over our actions; thereby preventing the approach of every unworthy thought and deed, thus preserving consciences void of offense toward God and man.[35]

In other words, the Tiler's sword should be used symbolically by all Freemasons to fend off the cowans in our minds: those ideas not fit for entry into the Temple of our lives. This deeply interior perspective reinforces the role that contemplation and self-reflection possess in the overall moral constitution of a Mason.

Vide, Aude, Tace

One of the old Latin mottos of the Masonic Order is *Vide, Aude, Tace*. It appears on eighteenth and nineteenth century engravings, frontispieces, degree patents, stone carvings and on many decorated items such as tankards.[36] The earliest definite date for its Masonic use may be its appearance in the frontispiece of the 1776 edition of the exposure, *Jachin and Boaz* (shown opposite), although it is likely older than that.

The motto is a series of three verbs in the imperative or "command" tense. *Vide* in Latin means "see" in both the literal sense and the figurative, and thus is connected to our words "visual" and "wit." The first refers only to the fact of seeing or not seeing something with our eyes, but the metaphorical meaning is clear in those moments of sudden understanding, when we naturally exclaim, "Ah, I see!"

Aude means "dare," and is the root of our word "audacity." A Mason must dare to apply to the Craft of his own free will and accord, and after he is initiated, it is his responsibility to embody such fortitude that he will be able to put the lessons of Freemasonry into practice. *Aude* follows *Vide* because there is no benefit from uninformed daring, nor from understanding without practical application.

Tace means "be silent," and is related to our words "tacit" and "taciturn." The command to remain silent may allude to the theme of Masonic silence in all of its dimensions: from the obligation that binds a Mason to his Craft, to the duty of every Mason to maintain in trust the secrets of his brethren. Some would even interpret this to imply a duty, incumbent upon all contemplative brethren, to preserve the Craft's esoteric wisdom from the abuses of the profane.

VIDE, AUDE, TACE.

5776.

California jewelry designer Andrew Horn's *Vide Aude Tace* ring, first sculpted in 2003, is one of his best selling pieces. As a departure from the sterility often seen in modern Masonic jewelry, Horn's more organic lines strongly inspire the wearer to remember both the theortical and the practical applications of lesson to "Know, Dare, and Be Silent."

All together, the motto literally means "See (or Understand), Dare, Be Silent," and its essence may be best expressed as "Understand It, Boldly Practice It, Remain Silent about It"—truly a fitting summary of the most important things required of a Masonic initiate.

The recent resurgence in the popularity of this motto in the United States may be partly traced to the often-expressed desires of younger Freemasons to see the dignity of the Craft elevated back to its former levels.[37] Of course, a similar motto has remained common in English Freemasonry, since the United Grand Lodge of England has prominently featured *Audi, Vide, Tace* ("Listen, Observe, Remain Silent") as its motto since 1813.[38]

Silence in the Ancient Temple

It is appropriate to point out that, as every tiled lodge is intended to represent the Temple of Solomon, the notion of maintaining silence in the lodge corresponds with traditional teachings about the Temple. It is not that the Jerusalem Temple and its environs would have been completely silent. There were psalms offered and sacrifices made, and on certain holidays great celebrations took place which would have been both joyous and loud. But at the inmost Temple precinct, as a matter of course, it was not at all acceptable to engage in any idle chatter or activity. The Temple's progressive series of walls and gates divided the sacred from the profane, the clean from the unclean.

Part of this division was the tradition of a respectful, sacred silence in the immediate vicinity of the altar and the sanctuary. As the prophet Habakkuk said over 2,600 years ago: "The LORD is in His holy temple: let all the earth keep silence before him." (2:20)

The priests were, apparently, careful to observe this discipline. There survives a very interesting first-person account of a visit to the Temple in Jerusalem around 200 BCE by a writer named Aristeas, who wrote to his brother:

> The Service of the priests is in every respect unsurpassed in the physical strength (required of them) and in its orderly and silent arrangement. For they all labour spontaneously, even though the exertion is great, and each one takes care of an appointed task. And they minister without a break, some offering the wood, some the oil, some the fine flour, some the incense, others the sacrificial portions of flesh, using their strength in different degrees for the different tasks. For [rest] there is a place where those who are relieved from duty sit down. When this happens, those who have rested rise up at the ready, since no one gives orders about matters of the Service. *And a complete silence reigns*, with the result that one might suppose that there was not a single person present in the place, even though there are around 700 ministering priests present and a great number of men bringing up the sacrifices; but everything is discharged with awe and in a manner worthy of the great Godhead. And I am certain that everyone who comes near to the sight of the things described above will come to astonishment and indescribable wonder, and will be stirred in mind by the holy quality which pertains to each detail.[39]

Aristeas, as an ancient traveler, was profoundly affected by what he saw in the Temple. And every experienced Mason knows that when we show similar respect for the work being done in our temples today, our "travelers" (that is, our candidates) are inspired with a similar wonder. When our officers know their roles and need no prompting, the work is much more powerful to see. Consistently doing so creates a space in which powerful and lasting impressions can be made, and in which the teachings of Freemasonry can be more clearly transmitted from each generation to the next.

Silence therefore is not emptiness. A deep and abiding silence is not a null or a void. It is a container, holding within it both the impressive words of our ceremonies and the often difficult to express wisdom that we may slowly come to perceive through our practice of Freemasonry. The first step toward this "deep silence" is a simple, unwavering respect for the correct flow of work within the lodge. A reverent atmosphere in the lodge could never do any harm. It will only take our work to a higher level, and allow us to register a deeper and more serious impression upon our candidates, members and visitors. Indeed, it will allow us — and the many we shall initiate — to begin to hear more acutely and understand more thoroughly the wisdom that was carefully implanted within our rites so many centuries ago. ☩

"Finally, silence, silence, silence, should be the first, second and third degrees of every man's Masonry."

M∴W∴ Bro∴ Abraham T. Metcalf
Grand Master of Masons in Michigan
1871

Notes

A highly abridged version of this paper appeared under the title "Multiple Dimensions of Silence in Freemasonry" in *The Journal of the Masonic Society*, Summer 2009, 5:23–26.

1. Stobaeus, fragment 24.
2. David Murray Lyon, *History of the Lodge of*

Edinburgh (Mary's Chapel) № 1. (London: Gresham Publishing Co., 1900), 451. Original orthography: "Wee ordaine lykwayes that no lodge be holden with-in a dwelling house wher ther is people living in it, but in the open fieldes except it be ill weather, and then Let ther be a house chosen that no person shall heir nor sie ws." The dating of the Aberdeen Mark Book, which contains this manuscript, is contested by scholar David Stevenson on the basis that it contains a membership list bearing names of several who could not have been members in 1670. However, the year 1670 as recorded on the membership list may be only decorative. There is no particular reason to doubt the date given on the Constitutions (a separate document in the same book); in fact, it could well be that the 1670 founding or re-constituting date given on the Constitutions was the reason that the number appears elsewhere in the book. For example, a list of graduates from a college in a current year might be marked with a year that was over century earlier. In this case, we instinctively know that this means the college was *founded* in 1872. Stevenson dates the book, or at least the membership list within it, to the 1690s. For his analysis, see David Stevenson, *The First Freemasons: Scotland's Early Lodges and their Members*, second edition (Edinburgh: Grand Lodge of Scotland, 2001), 126–41; and *The Origins of Freemasonry: Scotland's Century, 1590–1710* (Cambridge, UK: Cambridge University Press, 1988), 202–204. For photographs of selected pages from the Aberdeen Mark Book, see A.L. Miller, *Notes on the Early History and Records of the Lodge, Aberdeen 1ᵗᵉʳ* (Aberdeen: The University Press, 1919). The Mark Book is currently being prepared for a complete facsimile edition.

3. Ibid. Original orthography: "Wee ordaine lykwayes that none of our number shall whisper or round together in company with us without leave asked and given, all under the faylzie of the law of the Lodge or the will of the company." According to the *Dictionary of the Scots Langauge*, to "round" meant "To converse together (*sammyn, togidder*) in whispers; to

talk with or to a person privately or in whispers; to speak in a whisper." This dictionary is available at http://www.dsl.ac.uk/.

4. The first known speculative Freemasons in the New World were Quakers who were initiates of the Lodge at Aberdeen, and who settled in New Jersey in the 1680s. Some of these brethren experienced persecution and imprisonment in Scotland, but were welcomed within Freemasonry. See Stevenson, *The First Freemasons*, 138–45.

5. Stevenson, *Origins of Freemasonry*, 203.

6. If should be noted, however, that there is no proof that Anderson was a member of his father's lodge, although he did know of and was proud of his father's Masonic career. See David Stevenson, "James Anderson: Man & Mason," *Heredom: The Transactions of the Scottish Rite Research Society* 10 (2002): 94–96.

7. James Anderson, *The Constitutions of the Free-Masons* (London: J. Senex, 1723), 53–54. Similar to this is the note about the quarterly Grand Lodge communication: "[A]ll Matters that concern the *Fraternity* in general, or particular *Lodges*, or single Brethren, are quietly, sedately, and maturely to be discours'd of and transacted." (61)

8. Laurence Dermott, *Ahiman Rezon, or A Help to a Brother, Shewing the Excellency of Secrecy, and the First Cause, or Motive, of the Institution of Free-Masonry* (London: James Bedford, 1756), 30.

9. In addition to the clear regulations about maintaining silence during the labors of the lodge, the Antients' *Ahiman Rezon* teaches that after the Master's labors were complete, it was perfectly appropriate for him to join the brethren in drink, food and song: "And when thou hast done all thy Duty, sit down, that thou mayst be merry with them...." (xv)

10. This is a crucial point. If the brethren were typically boisterous and drunk during the initiations, we would expect the exposures to capitalize upon it. Instead, they tend to describe drinking taking place before or (generally) after initiations. *Three Distinct Knocks* (London: H. Serjeant, 1760), for example, describes the procedure for closing the lodge, ending

with: "then they take off their Jewels, and get as drunk as Free-masons may be; and sing and get drunk and that's all &c." (39) *Jachin and Boaz* (London: W. Nicholl, 1762) describes the set-up and opening of London's Modern lodges as follows: "When they sit down to the Table, the Master seats himself in the first Place on the East-Side, the Bible being opened before him, with the Compasses laid thereon, and the Points of them covered with the Lignum Vitæ or Box Square; and the Senior and Junior Wardens opposite to him on the West and South. On the Table is likewise placed different Sorts of Wine, Punch, &c. to regale the Brethren, who take their Places according to their Degree or Seniority. Being thus seated, after a few Minutes, the Master proceeds to *open the Lodge* in the following Manner." (4–5) The account describes the lodge being opened at table, at which point the Master makes a statement "forbidding all Cursing, Swearing, or Whispering, and all profane Discourse whatever," after which "they sit down, and drink promiscuously [i.e., without specific leave asked of the Master—Ed.], or take a Pipe of Tobacco." (6–7) Soon after, however, if there was a candidate for the degrees, the lodge members would leave their seats. While the candidate was sitting for half an hour in the dark silence of the Chamber of Reflection (7), the others re-arranged things in "the Grand Apartment" as necessary for the initiation, including "drawing the…Figure [lodge board] on the Floor at the upper Part of the Room." (8) As described by *Jachin and Boaz*, the entire initiation ceremony took place around this drawing, not at the table where the refreshments were (8–12). After the initiation, it says that "The Brethren now congratulate the new-made Member, and all *return to the Table to regale themselves*; when the Master proposes a Health to the young Brother, which is drank with the greatest Applause by the whole Body…." (12–13, emphasis added) More drinking and toasts would continue through the night. So, a close reading reveals that lodges aimed to balance revelry and solemnity, providing opportunities for the enjoyment and preservation of both.

11. The Latin phrase *Funde merum genio* means

"Pour a wine offering to your Genius"—*genius*, of course, understood in the ancient sense of one's *daimon* or intrinsic spirit. Such libations were offered on one's birthday (cf. Censorius, *De Die Natali Liber* 2.1–3); in the Masonic usage, its connection to the Apprentice's obligation would indicate that it commemorated one's initiation as a "Masonic birthday."

12. Apparently, this toast was familiar both in Antient and Modern settings. It is found in *Three Distinct Knocks* (a 1760 exposure purportedly of the practices of the Antients), 20, and *Jachin and Boaz* (a 1762 exposure of the Moderns), 17. To see that this was not done after the obligation in the initiation ritual itself, compare *Jachin and Boaz*, pages 12 and 17. Confusion between these two sections has contributed to some scholars suggesting that the early initiations may have included such toasts (cf. Bernard E. Jones, *The Freemasons' Guide and Compendium*, 478). Other scholars have pointed out the distinction between the actual initiation and the rehearsal of the lecture (cf. J.M. Harvey, "Initiation Two Hundred Years Ago," *Ars Quatuor Coronatorum* 75 (1962): 217.) The fact that the *Funde merum genio* was not done immediately after the obligation *in cæremonia* is worthy, if not conclusive, evidence that the Brethren were not drinking wine during the actual ceremony. *Three Distinct Knocks* is clear that the central area of the lodge is occupied during the ritual by a chalk or tape drawing (the lodge plan). After the obligation, this is erased, and "[t]hen a Table is put in the Place where this Figure was, and they all sit round it; but every Man sitteth in the same Place as he stood before the Figure was washed out…. Every Man has a Glass set him, and a large Bowl of Punch, or what they like, is set in the Center of the Table…." (11).

13. Reprinted in Wellins Calcott, *A Candid Disquisition* (London: James Dixwell, 1769), 118.

14. W.L. Wilmshurst, *The Masonic Initiation*, Revised Edition (San Francisco: Plumbstone, 2007), 30–31.

15. "Such symbolic or emblematic figures and their attributes were frequently codified in the later medieval and renaissance periods." Philip Ward-Jackson, *Public Sculpture of the*

City of London (Liverpool: Liverpool University Press, 2003), 441.

16. John Bancks, *Miscellaneous Works, in Verse and Prose, of Mr. John Bancks* (London: James Hodges, 1739), 1:37.

17. Lesley Adkins & Roy A. Adkins, *Dictionary of Roman Religion* (New York: Facts on File, 1996), 9, 242–43.

18. *Naturalis Historia* 3.9.

19. Ibid.

20. Laurence Dermott, *Ahiman Rezon, or A Help to a Brother* (London: James Bedford, 1756), 7.

21. For example, the 1805 first American edition of Dermott's *Ahiman Rezon* and James Hardie's *Monitor* (New York, 1819). The actual classical phrase was *digito compesce labellum*, as given in Juvenal, *Satires* 1.160.

22. Calcott, *Candid Disquisitions*, 51; William Preston, *Illustrations of Masonry* (London: J. Wilkie, 1772), 175; William Hutchinson, *The Spirit of Masonry*, second edition (Carlisle: F. Jollie, 1795), 283.

23. William Fringham, *Hieroglyphica*, 1755. See a reproduction of part of this image on p. 85. The same gesture frequently appears on eighteenth-century Master Mason certificates.

24. Horace, *Odes* 3.2.25–28. Horace is specifically referring to the ritual secrecy of the Eleusinian mysteries, as the passage continues: "Never would I allow one who has profaned the mysteries of Ceres to stay with me beneath the same roof, nor to set sail with me in the same fragile ship." Author's translation.

25. Albert G. Mackey, *An Encyclopædia of Freemasonry and Its Kindred Sciences* (Philadelphia: Moss & Co., 1879), vol. 1, 70.

26. Around 1820 William Rush, the first great American sculptor, was hired to produce many works of art for the Grand Lodge of Pennsylvania, including sculptures of the two Cherubim (adapted from the design of the Antients' coat of arms), and allegorical figures of Faith, Hope, Charity and Silence. See *William Rush: American Sculptor* (Philadelphia: Pennsylvania Academy of Fine Arts, 1982), 159–64. A note in *The Freemason's Monitor* by Z. A. Davis (Philadelphia: Desilver & Muir, 1843) specifically identifies Rush's *Silence* as a statue of Angerona (p. 126).

27. Commissioned by the Grand Lodge of New York and sculpted by the famous artist Augustus Saint-Gaudens in 1874. This Angerona, perhaps the finest of them all, stood at the main staircase in the Grand Temple from 1876 until it was removed to the New York Masonic Hospital in Utica in 1923. See John H. Dryfhout,

◄ *Silence*, by Augustus Saint Gaudens, completed in 1874. Property of the Grand Lodge F∴& A∴M∴, State of New York. Photo: Richard J. Powell.

The Work of Augustus Saint-Gaudens (Hanover, N.H.: University Press of New England, 2008), 75.

28. Colin Dyer, "The Radford and Tunnah Manuscripts and their Relationship with Other Pre-Union Lectures," *Ars Quatuor Coronatorum* 88(1975), 59.

29. Dyer, "Radford and Tunnah Manuscripts," 62.

30. Charles Whitlock Moore (Ed.), *The Freemason's Monthly Magazine*, vol. 1 (1842), 85.

31. For a further exploration of this, see Shawn Eyer, "To Stand in the Symbolic Center," *Ad Lucem* 16(2009): 11–29. (*Ad Lucem* is a private journal of the Societas Rosicruciana in Civitatibus Fœderatis.) For a detailed examination of Edward George Bulwer-Lytton's connection to the S.R.I.A., see R.A. Gilbert, "'The Supposed Rosy Crucian Society': Bulwer-Lytton and the S.R.I.A." In *Ésotérisme, Gnoses & Imaginaire Symbolique: Mélanges Offerts à Antoine Faivre*, edited by Richard Caron, Jocelyn Godwin, Wouter J. Hanegraaff & Jean-Louis Vieillard (Leuven: Peeters, 2001), 389–402.

32. Colin Dyer, *William Preston and His Work* (Shepperton, UK: Lewis Masonic, 1987), 175.

33. William Preston, *Illustrations of Masonry*, Second Edition (London: J. Wilkie, 1775), 173.

34. Jeremy Ladd Cross, *The True Masonic Chart, or Hieroglyphic Monitor* (New York: J. L. Cross, 1850), 39.

35. Charles Whitlock Moore & S. W. B. Carnegy, *The Masonic Trestle-board* (Boston: C. W. Moore, 1846), 77.

36. For some examples see T. O. Haunch, "English Craft Certificates," *Ars Quatuor Coronatorum* 82(1969): 189; John D. Hamilton, *Material Culture of the American Freemasons* (Lexington, Mass.: Museum of Our National Heritage, 1994), 219; W. Kirk MacNulty, *Freemasonry: A Journey Through Ritual and Symbol* (London: Thames & Hudson, 1991), 69.

37. An example of the renewed interest in this traditional Masonic motto is the popular ring designed by Bro∴ Andrew Horn in 2003, featuring the words *Vide Aude Tace* as its central motif and inspiration.

38. This is a shortened form of the Medieval couplet, *Audi, vide, tace, si vis vivere in pace* ("Listen, look, be silent, if you wish to live in peace.") This version of the motto appears in Masonic evidence as early as 1777. See Haunch, "English Craft Certificates," 189n.

39. Letter of Aristeas §§ 92, 94–95, 99. Translation and commentary in C. T. R. Hayward, *The Jewish Temple: A Non-Biblical Sourcebook* (London: Routledge, 1996), 26–37.

▶ Allegorical statue of Silence from the grand atrium of the Scottish Rite Temple in Guthrie, Oklahoma. Photo: Thomas J. Monteforte.

First Initiation · *Mounir Hanafi*

What courage Diogenes had
walking with his midday
   lantern in hand,
searching for truth and light.

Unlearning this and that
And later reincarnating
   into the slim frame
of an Idiot, that Sufi Saint Nazurudeen.
Searching, always searching for the key
of it all
   forgetting the lock—
since as of late he knew
   that any device might do.

Who walks without any chains,
   on unfamiliar terrain,
   blindfolded
led by a man he does not even know?
What yearning, nostalgia, sense
   of coming home could bring a man to such
  a state.

There is in the East a Light behind the light.
There is a path some stumble upon—
   others remember, was a passion
   of a father, grandfather, uncle or older
   brother—
and there, letting go of all control,
   they in tandem kneel and pray
that the secret of their souls
   becomes revealed.

Can you imagine walking out from Plato's
   cave
where just a shadow is what you knew as the
   dawn?
Can you imagine looking at the Sun
   created by
            One
incomprehensibly and infinitely
   brighter then the brightest light?

Can you imagine meeting your Creator Face
   to face,
like blessed Jacob on the bank of the Jabbok?
Remember him, and look to the old pilgrims
   who guide us even now,
retracing steps from ancient myths—
   until finally there you are,
   you stand alone.
You kneel,
   and at last are brought
         to Light.

Jabbok

Erik O'Neal

T HE CAMPFIRES flickered on the south bank stabbing long fiery replicas at him over the water. Jacob stood alone, detached from his tribe. He stretched his stiffening body and combed his beard with his fingers. He rarely afforded himself such isolation. He sat cross-legged in the dust and looked up at the clear constellations. For a moment he felt like a boy again keeping watch in the hilly pastures of the South.

But, here the Jabbok was not so wide that Jacob could not hear the faint din of the newly made camp. There was the usual rumpus from the livestock, the squealing of children and barking of dogs. Men were heard shouting over the whole commotion, but their words disintegrated in the air, subverted by the swift water hissing through the reeds.

Jacob's people forded that day without incident. Every lamb was accounted for, and a great gift of tribute was being prepared for Esau who traveled at that very moment with a host of men to meet Jacob. What would come to pass at that reunion? Even in this almost restful time, dread was in Jacob's heart. He remembered his brother's face, ruddy and earnest. Esau was a natural man, close to the spirits of the field, a chieftain of the oldest sort. Jacob wondered how he could ever have dominion over such a man. He thought of turning back to Haran.

But, Laban's abuses still scraped him, and hate for his father-in-law was bitter in Jacob's mouth. He fantasized that Esau might greet him warmly, and even as he crawled before Esau in supplication, his mystified brother would simply laugh, having forgotten the ancient slight. Naturally, the long awaited reunion with their father and mother in Canaan would have to wait. Esau would first insist that after a hearty feast here on the banks of the river Jabbok, the sons of Isaac would come to Haran and take revenge on the villains there. Jacob savored the vision of Laban squirming in terror before the united tribe of Abraham.

A long croak, perhaps that of a heron, erupted from a nearby bed of reeds, shattering Jacob's fantasy. Something akin to a laugh escaped his throat. He thought now of Laban and his allies wetting themselves with glee at the prospect of massacring his sad lot of scrawny nomads.

But, Esau would never come with him to Haran. Jacob now envisioned his estranged brother rushing out to meet him, taking him in a mighty fraternal embrace, and at once stabbing out his heart. Jacob stared at the darkness, his thoughts leaked from his mouth.

"Or, he might spear me as I lie begging in the dust at his feet."

The tang of the campfires crossed over on the southern wind. The presently lesser son of Isaac stretched out his legs and leaned back on his palms, fingering the sandy earth. A thin crescent moon climbed patiently over the thick wild oaks. In those years at *Paddan-Aram*, Jacob's herd multiplied and his noble wives gave exceptional progeny, but his heart was destitute. Jacob contemplated the actions which brought him to exile. How could Esau begrudge him such a 'blessing?' If indeed that is the word for it. Jacob dared not call it by its true name. He would not openly brand it a curse, risking it to blasphemy. Should the middle chamber of a man's life be so hard won? The emptiness of that chamber consumed Jacob. His was a house grown fat on the swallowed pride of its master, and much want showed in Jacob's thin bones.

After all, what did he take from his brother? In fact, Esau kept his birthright and premier status well in hand. In terms of worldly chattels Esau's wealth was greater. What did Isaac's promises amount to? Were that timid old man's words worthy to make a liar and a thief of Jacob? He might very well have stolen the air from between Esau's toes.

Isaac and Rebecca filled their sons with stories of Abraham and the legacy that would one day fall upon them. Jacob wondered if Isaac really thought himself a king always negotiating with some neighborhood tyrant for a few paddocks of grass and squabbling with every redneck shepherd they meet over fresh water. In this capacity Esau was just the man for the job, all the time leading his race to more verdant meadows, offering a fitting sacrifice to each and every fiendish deity along the way.

At first, he blamed it on his mother's avarice, but Jacob knew his own ambition. In his dreams the people of Abraham raise a civilization, and wizened chiefs approach the radiance of their cities desiring to pitch tents and graze their flocks thereabouts. Jacob knew that he must be more than a good son and a great father to create such a boon for his people. A nation as numerous as the stars in the sky and the dust of the Earth requires a great sire, an instrument of Divine Will.

From the darkness an owl issued a desolate shriek. Jacob's dreams abandoned him, leaving him alone again on the fine sands of the Jabbock. An apprehension loitered in the back of his mind, something that transcended the predicament at hand. There were promises made at the place Jacob called *Beth-El*. Were his people forsaken? Could the One who stood beside him there on the road to Haran prove a delusion? Surely, no one stood with Jacob now. He agonized about the covenant that was his to keep. Although, his sons and each man in his clan were circumcised in the correct manner, the devotion of Jacob's people to one inimitable Divinity before all others was all but superficial. He suspected his own wife of carrying away Laban's household idols. He well knew her purpose. The master's feigned ignorance of the profane traditions kept in his house and the ritual conducted in the nearby groves made him complicit.

The wind shifted, the strong scent of oleander drifted down the Northern bank. The son of Isaac all but swooned, suddenly struck with a nauseous sensation. His jaw tightened, setting his teeth to shatter. The lights and sounds of the camp on the far bank withered away, the slender moon gave out, and the mighty stars dimmed. The luxurious Jabbok roared. The son of Isaac clasped his hands over his ears. But, as swiftly as it came, the sickness passed and all was silent. Jacob, gaining his feet, found himself engulfed in a heavy gloom. In the blackness he perceived a figure approaching on two feet, a man. Jacob called out angrily.

"Do you come again for your little gods, Laban?"

In fact a fight was in Jacob's heart when the thing came upon him there. He expected to kill Laban. Jacob looked hard at the advancing form, but could not distinguish its face.

"Is that my father-in-law? What devilry is this?"

Then there came a blow. Jacob fell hard on his back. It was on him like an immense cat, battering him viciously. Jacob raised his hands to shield himself, only to have both of his wrists seized in one great hand. Like a sadistic father preparing to tickle a child, the thing put its full weight on Jacob's legs and with its free hand gripped his face. Bewildered, Jacob writhed desperately struggling to free himself from the weight of the assailant.

Jacob knew this was no man. He cried out in terror, but the words clotted in his mouth. The thing raised up its fist for a ruinous strike. Jacob closed his eyes, expecting to die.

The blow drove Jacob deep into darkness. The earth dissolved away leaving him to roil in the furious black ether. He perceived the thickening of time and his senses deserted him utterly. He knew the Being was with him. Jacob imparted his thoughts.

"Where am I?"

The Being expressed amusement.

"This is your world unclothed, a contraction of truth."

"Was it you who stood beside me on the road from Luz, the place I call Beth-El?"

"You can not flatter me, Jacob."

Jacob's eyes were open, but he saw nothing, only the ineffable things we see in total blackness.

"Will you destroy me?"

"In time."

"What of my family? Will they be slaughtered?"

"Already, you know their fate."

"I don't understand."

"It was told, they will match the dust of the earth and the stars in the sky. Do you doubt this?"

Jacob tried to put his hands together in supplication, but one could not find the other in the void.

"I have sinned greatly."

The Being laughed at Jacob.

"You are more than a match for Laban in that respect."

"Yes."

"And what has your infamous guile bought you?

"Nothing... nothing. "

The Being gave no response. It was some time before it spoke again.

"What do you desire?"

"You know my dreams."

"Have you reflected upon what you saw on the road to Haran?"

"I sometimes dream of the staircase, but as I make the ascent, the way before me is concealed."

"You never know what is coming, Jacob, and when it comes, it is never so pretty as in your dreams.

"They are black of late."

"Where better to know the light than in dark place?"

Jacob attempted no reply.

"What did you expect to find here?"

"I can not say."

Jacob stared into the nothingness that surrounded him. No one spoke for a long time. Jacob thought he could discern a single point of light from deep within the darkness. And one by one the stars were revealed in the void.

"Do you see them?"

"Yes. I see their light, but they are always silent."

The Being laughed again.

"You do not hear the Master?"

"Only in dreams"

"Abraham, he too, is long silent, but his light is within you, Jacob. Does it not speak to you?"

"Yes, I suppose, after a fashion."

The Master is grateful to Abraham, he had much to teach."

"I do not understand."

"The children of Abraham are blessed and will multiply. But whether they blow like dust about the world making shadow and filling cracks or shimmer like the stars is up to you."

"Is it in my power, Master?"

"The fate of your race is yours to rule. Bend it to your Will. Reserve your cunning for something more than crude acquisitions and easy indulgences, Jacob. You are the master of your dreams. It is by Will alone that these formless notions can be manifested."

The stars rotated in the sky as the sublime thing spun on its heels. Jacob knew that it held him in its arms like a child. They had returned and the dawn was coming. The thing placed Jacob's body on the ground. It spoke.

"I must leave you now."

Jacob gripped its ankle with both hands.

"Wait!"

The thing looked down at him, but Jacob trembled in its gaze. He dared not look at the face. He spoke to the dust.

"I wish to know your name. What is your name, Lord, so that we may honor you?"

"My name? Indeed, so that you might conjure me. It is of no use to you."

The thing attempted to step away and depart, but found itself fixed to that spot, held fast by Jacob.

"I can not release you, lest, from here I advance with your blessing."

"Would you pull my leg, little man? I would think you tired of blessings."

The thing knelt down and touched Jacob's right thigh. A burning heat passed through him. He knew nothing like it. His mind flashed white, and he screamed in agony. The thing laughed.

"So that you remember me."

Jacob clutched his injured limb, tears coursed down his cheeks. The thing blessed him.

"More life you will have. More as it has been, and Great Light if you choose to pursue it. Advance, you are blessed."

Jacob stood, his damaged leg quivered. With the other he took a single step and stood before the Divine thing.

"I would not break you for it is known that you do not bend. When your brother comes, he will know by your step that you are called Israel."

"Will we meet again, another night?"

"Surely. I am ever in the corner of your eye." ✦

To each true and faithful heart
That still preserves the Secret Art—
Tho' disapproves the world,
And says "There's nothing there."

The Mason knows: the Craft's alive;
The honey, gold within the hive,
Sweet and secret, saved alone
For ones who live by Plumb and Square.

To the true and faithful heart of
the regular Mason!

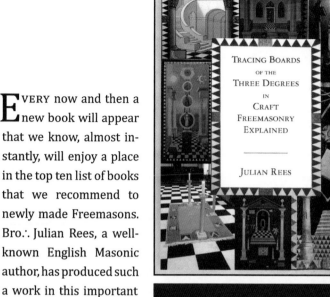

TRACING BOARDS
OF THE
THREE DEGREES
IN
CRAFT
FREEMASONRY
EXPLAINED

———

JULIAN REES

Reviewed by Shawn Eyer

EVERY now and then a new book will appear that we know, almost instantly, will enjoy a place in the top ten list of books that we recommend to newly made Freemasons. Bro∴ Julian Rees, a well-known English Masonic author, has produced such a work in this important new book on the tracing boards—a subject of great interest to all students of the meaning and development of the Craft's symbolism.

This is a volume long needed. For many years, the best way to study the tracing boards at home has been to obtain the rightly beloved Masonic art books of W. Kirk MacNulty—*Freemasonry: A Journey Through Ritual and Symbol* (1991) and *Freemasonry: Symbols, Secrets, Significance* (2006)—and read them alongside Terence Haunch's learned historical survey, *Tracing Boards: Their Development and Their Designers* (2004). Together, these books provide high quality examples of the boards, along with historical and interpretive commentary.

But Haunch's book is difficult to locate in the

◄ An Entered Apprentice board by Arthur Thistleton for the Ivanhoe Lodge in Leicestersire, 1836. This is especially notable for its orderly geometrical arrangement and its interesting placement of Jacob's Ladder. It is similar to a John Harris design of 1820.

United States, so while American Masons often enjoy seeing the occasional reproduction of tracing boards in various media, too commonly we have failed to actually study them in depth. This is a shame, because, with few exceptions, the images on the tracing boards apply just as readily to our contemplations as to the reflections of our brethren in England and in other lands where such boards are commonly used.

There is a popular misconception that the tracing boards are mere devices meant to assist us in the ritualistic performance of the memorized lectures. While these images may be very helpful as mnemonic tools, Rees traces the real origins of the tracing boards to some of the most essential psychological needs of man, most importantly the urge to create "in a form comprehensible to his fellow men...images that would assist him in devotion to the deity." Thus, within Freemasonry, the boards serve to help us better convey the inner meaning of the ritual.

In further discussion of this matter, Rees demonstrates that the boards hearken back to a time when a much greater level of instruction was imparted to the candidate. He includes, for example, the tracing board-style frontispiece of a 1766 exposure, along with its original accompanying text, which delineates each symbol in the engraving, and then concludes: "The Uses of the above Materials are fully defined in the Course of the Work, both spiritually and temporally." This is good evidence that lectures and orations on symbolism were frequently given in lodges before Preston's system of lectures were developed. It also indicated that—in some cases—they were meant to explain the tracing boards.

After reminding us that there exist eighteenth century records that describe initiates studying drawings made directly on the lodge room floor (which were, due to their esoteric nature, washed away immediately after the temple was closed), Rees reveals his view of the important role the tracing boards can play:

Freemasonry is about rendering in symbol and allegory that which words alone cannot render. And a visual image gives us a way of using our own insight to decode the message. The tracing boards are there to do just that—from their original function of laying out the plan of the building, they have developed into a means for us to lay out the message, and then to profit by it.

In order that the reader might so profit, the book features good reproductions (mostly in color) of eighty-one tracing boards, in addition to some supporting illustrations. Several of the boards are reproduced at a large size, nearly filling the page. The majority are given in smaller dimensions, but the halftone quality is general-

◀ The final version of John Harris' Fellow Craft board, painted in 1849. The Winding Staircase is relocated, and Harris has also introduced a cameo of Solomon exhibiting the Temple to the Queen of Sheba, an allusion to the ritual of the Board of Installed Masters. Solomon's gesture to the staircase recalls the ancient tradition that "when the queen of Sheba had seen all Solomon's wisdom, and the house that he had built... and his ascent by which he went up unto the house of the LORD...she said to the king, It was a true report that I heard in mine own land of thy acts and of thy wisdom." (1 Kings 10.4–6)

▶ The rare 1850 version of Harris' third degree board, showing the open grave of the slain Master Hiram. The board is marked by a marble monument featuring many symbols. Here, the Hebrew enscription, which later copyists would turn into gibberish, is intact. It reads: "The House of the Temple in Jerusalem was built under Solomon the King of Israel, Hiram the King of Tyre, and Hiram of the tribe of Naphtali, the builders, in the year 3000."

◀ A contemporary tracing board by Bro∴ Ferenc Sebök, a Belgian painter, made for the Quadrum Leonardi Lodge in Budapest. This board shows the strong influence of modern art upon the Apprentice tableau, particularly in the vigorous depiction of the lunar and solar elements. Here, the relentless linear order of the Mosaic Pavement is dramatically juxaposed against a swirling maelstrom of symbols and archetypes. Some of the familiar symbolism is simplified and transformed—for example, the four tassells of the border have become two drooping lotus flowers. The Blazing Star is replaced by the Point within the Circle—with the point itself represented by the Hebrew letter י (*yud*), suggesting a degree of kabbalistic influence.

ly clear enough for us to study the details. Some of the design decisions seem pragmatic. For example, Josiah Bowring's extremely influential and beautiful E∴A∴, F∴C∴ and M∴M∴ tracing boards are given only in small size, but this is no doubt owing to the fact that they are reproduced so beautifully in W. Kirk MacNulty's books. This has allowed room for a significant number of boards that have never appeared in print before, or never before in color. Their presence here is very welcome.

The excellent artistic value of the book is complimented by Julian Rees' insightful commentary upon the three Craft tracing boards. These essays are concise but sophisticated, and possess the kind of flexibility and depth of thought that is clearly the result of many decades' exploration of the Craft rituals.

A fine example of this fluid interpretation is found in his discussion of the second degree. In the English Emulation Rite, the Fellow Craft is taken to the Southeast corner of the Lodge, and told that he is "now permitted to extend [his] researches into the hidden mysteries of nature and science." Many have expressed confusion about what this might mean, but Rees has an engaging way to address the matter:

You may ask, since when were 'nature' and 'science' mysteries? And why should they be hidden? If we shift our perspective, and think of nature as our *own* nature, and think of science as the *knowing* of that nature, and consider then that self-knowledge follows from our uncovering, *dis*covering our own nature which may be hidden under layers of impediments which modern life lays on it, then we gain enlightenment enabling a richer view.

The author's interest in philosophical matters is obvious, and his essays occasionally refer to Hermetic and mystical topics. He demonstrates how several of the symbols in the Apprentice board denote the "interconnection of celestial and terrestrial," with Jacob's Ladder "being an emblem of the possibility of man's ascent to celestial realms." In discussing the lessons of the third degree, Rees again emphasizes that a Mason's journey is an interior one:

> Heaving learned to know ourselves, discovered our own vital and immortal principle, named the spark of divinity within ourselves, we can indeed ensure the triumph of good over evil.

After his main section using the "standard" boards of the Emulation working to illuminate the Craft degrees, Ress includes two more sections: one on history and variations of the boards, and one on the use of tracing boards outside the United Grand Lodge of England. These chapters are filled with very interesting and artistic variations upon the more familiar tracing board themes, including the work of the Belgian painter and composer, Ferenc Sebők.

Tracing Boards of the Three Degrees in Craft Freemasonry Explained is a book that many in the Craft have looked forward to. By bringing to life the rich iconography of this critical part of our material culture, Julian Rees has enabled a new generation of Freemasons to gain insight into their traditions and the development thereof. Thanks to Rees, American Masons need no longer admire the tracing boards from afar.

As a work of historical scholarship, it is sound but not academically rigorous. As such, T. O. Haunch's monograph (or his original 1963 *AQC* article on the subject) will remain essential reading for scholars of the boards. For the general reader, however, Rees' *Tracing Boards* is now the obvious choice for the average Masonic reader who would like to begin exploring the meaning of these stimulting works of art.

*Tracing Boards of the Three Degrees
  in Craft Freemasonry Explained*
Julian Rees
96 pp., Lewis Masonic, 2009
ISBN 978-0-85318-334-1
softcover $22.95 US   £12.99 UK   ⨎

THE TRACING BOARD is an emblem of the book of nature
with all the designs of Infinite Wisdom,
drawn and delineated by the Supreme Architect of the
Universe which, though he who runs may read,
the Mason who contemplates
will dare to imitate and pursue the plans
which will ensure present and lead to eternal happiness.
— William Preston, 1772

I CAME ACROSS this excellent book in 2004 at the suggestion of a friend of mine living in Japan. Though both involved in spiritual pursuits, he had already received his Masonic initiation and I had not; his recommendation started a journey that resulted in my own initiation into the Craft.

Prior to the SUNY version, now widely available, one could only obtain the book via the University of Göteborg or through occasional copies sold by Ben Fernee's Caduceus Books in London. The SUNY version omits fifteen figures found in the original; both editions contain the same illustrative tables.

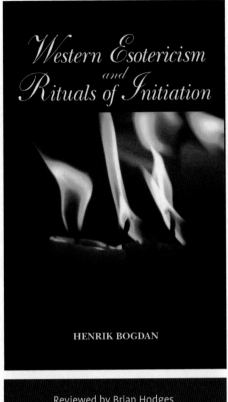

Western Esotericism
and
Rituals of Initiation

HENRIK BOGDAN

Reviewed by Brian Hodges

ventions such as Christianity; she maintained this tradition provided momentum for what became the scientific revolution.

On the other hand, Faivre's approach considers Western esotericism as a "form of thought" based on several factors: symbolic correspondences between tangible phenomena and mystical forces; "living nature", or nature as a network of mystical linkages, influencing and influenced by subtle operations; the fundamental role of imagination in acquiring sacred wisdom; the concept of transmutation; synthesis of the common denominators from many philosophical and esoteric traditions, such as Neoplatonism, Gnosticism, Hermeticism, etc., into one "concordance;" and the impartation of occult knowledge from master to student via formal operations and rules.

Please note that throughout this review I will use the word *masonic* to refer to Bogdan's definition of 'masonic initiatory societies' and *Masonic* to refer to modern regular Craft as practiced in the US and elsewhere.

Bogdan introduces the book with an exploration of the academic basis for his investigation and his methodological approach, which seeks to place "masonic initiation" within a historical and contextual framework. In other words, one must view "Western esotericism" as a phenomenon relative to its place in history. He follows this with a survey of the primary researchers on the topic: Dame Francis Yates, Antoine Faivre, and Wouter Hanegraaff.

Francis Yates' theories in the 1960s focus on the Hermetic tradition as a self-contained, discrete and parallel tradition to formal mainstream con-

Hanegraaff quibbles with Faivre's definitions but does not argue their essential viability; he contends that Faivre focuses on the esotericism of the Renaissance, which does not take into account how esotericism changes throughout time (and continues to do so). He asserts that it should be thought of as a complex, changing concept. He also critiques the details of Faivre's components without negating them: for example, the symbolic correspondences noted above experienced significant change after the scientific revolution (hence post-Renaissance); this colors our understanding of it when viewed from a nineteenth (or twenty-first) century perspective.

Turning to an analysis of ritual, Bogdan considers Arnold van Gennep, whose important work *Les Rites de Passage* (Rites of Passage) breaks down initiation rituals into three phases: separation, transition and incorporation. Rites of separation take an initiate from one group or experience to another; rites of transition focus on changing the mindset in order to facilitate operating in the new environment; and rites of incorporation reinforce the new set of prescribed behavior or viewpoint in the resulting group. Victor Turner, who focuses on transition rites as the "liminal phase," points out that in this phase the initiate receives sacred knowledge or gnosis and often features the symbolic death of the initiate.

The next section provides the historical framework for the development of Western esoteric thought. From the rediscovery of the Corpus Hermeticum to Neoplatonism and Kabbalah, Bogdan details the investigations of John Dee, particularly in his *Monas Hieroglyphica*, Marcelo Ficino and Giordano Bruno. He then turns to the emergence of the Rosicrucian myth via early documents such as the *Fama Fraternitatis* and *The Chemical Wedding of Christian Rosenkreutz* to set the stage for the emergence of masonic societies. Bogdan then gets into the meat of "masonic initiation rituals," the basis of "masonic initiatory societies," into which he includes not only the familiar Craft and Scottish Rite lodges but also bodies deriving from the Hermetic Order of the Golden Dawn and modern Wicca. He adds those latter two categories not as a means to validate them as Freemasonic organizations, but rather to acknowledge their reliance on inherently masonic characteristics embedded in their initiatory rites.

Bogdan begins his examination of Freemasonry with James Anderson's *The Constitutions of the Free-Masons*. Published in 1723, the *Constitutions* draw heavily from the Old Charges, medieval documents that formed the link between operative and speculative Freemasonry. Interestingly, Bogdan explores the supposed connection between Rosicrucianism and Freemasonry at some length, delving into the myth espoused by several that Freemasonry derived from the R.+C.

In any case, by the 1730 publication of Pritchard's *Masonry Dissected*, the masonic initiatory system had moved from two to three degrees familiar to the Craft today: Entered Apprentice, Fellow Craft and Master Mason. Basing his findings on the publication of Masonic exposés, Bogdan demonstrates that the degrees went through two periods of development: from the late 1730s to the early 1750s, in France, where degrees became more elaborate and began to include passwords and tracing boards; and from the 1760s through the end of the eighteenth century, in England, where the lodges placed increasing emphasis on securing their proceedings from outsiders via passwords, ritual formula and a reversal of the words associated with each degree. He makes an important assertion here: that the third degree Hiramic legend has an association with the Kabbalistic notion of the search for the lost word. Drawing upon Jan Snoek's analysis of the *Zohar*, a seminal Kabbalist text, he demonstrates that the ability to pronounce the word — the Tetragrammaton of the Kabbalists or the "Lost Word" of Masonry — demonstrates an influence of Kabbalah on masonic ritual, one of the few such direct influences of esoteric traditions upon the Craft degrees.

He sees further evidence of more direct esoteric inspiration in the higher degrees, especially in the Ecossais and Templar Rites found within the Scottish Rite, focusing in particular on the 18th and 28th degrees, Knight of the Rose-Croix and

Knight of the Sun respectively, as well as other degrees with alchemical symbolism. Bogdan also investigates ever more esoteric degree systems formed in this period, along with their individual histories, adherents and characteristics. This includes the Strict Observance and its replacement in 1782 by the Rectified Scottish Rite, still active today; the Swedish Rite, which also remains active; and the so-called "Egyptian degrees" of Memphis and Mizraim. He continues with a survey of two degree systems no longer in use: the Rite Ecossais Philosophique and Der Orden des Gold-und Rosenkreuzes, both of which contained specific alchemical symbolism and knowledge passed on to its members in strict confidence. He also provides an example of the degree of Le Vrai Maçon or "True Mason," the fourth degree from the Rite Ecossais Philosophique, replete with alchemical imagery and symbolism explained in its lecture section.

Bogdan also provides an interesting survey of the ritual structure of the Hermetic Order of the Golden Dawn, a nineteenth-century magical order formed by Masons in London, which included in its membership the poet Yeats, S. L. MacGregor Mathers, Arthur Machen, and at one point Aleister Crowley. Its degrees featured obvious Masonic influence, as did its costumes, implements and regalia, but the Golden Dawn went much further into explicit kabbalistic and alchemical lessons. It had a tremendous influence on Western esoteric bodies throughout the period and continues as a baseline or template for groups being developed in the twenty-first century.

In conclusion, Bogdan has provided an important contribution to Masonic studies. By placing Freemasonry in its historical context relative to other manifestations of the Western esoteric tradition, he finds important correspondences between certain Masonic themes and esoteric gnosis, such as the relation between the Hiramic legend and the Kabbalistic search for pronunciation of the lost word, the relevance of death and resurrection themes and the influence of occult topics such as alchemy, astrology and magic upon Craft and higher degrees of masonry in the past and leading up to the present day. His exploration of Masonically-influenced esoteric groups, such as the Golden Dawn and the Gardnerian ceremonies, demonstrate that Masonic initiation rituals have influenced many other ritual societies that exist today.

Western Esotericism and Rituals of Initiation
Henrik Bogdan
235 pp., State Univ. of New York Press, 2007
ISBN 978-0-7914-7069-5
hardcover $66.00 US
ISBN 978-0-7914-7070-1
softcover $21.95 US

(Previously published as *From Darkness to Light: Western Esoteric Rituals of Initiation*. Göteborg University Department of Religious Studies, Sweden, 2003. ISBN 91-88348-30-X) ⚓

About the Contributors

Erik L. Arneson is a Past Master of Ashland Lodge № 23, A∴F∴ & A∴M∴ of Oregon.

Robert G. Davis is a Past Master of Guildhall Lodge № 553 in Stillwater, Oklahoma.

Laurence Dermott (1720–1791) was an Irish Freemason who became best known as the longtime Grand Secretary of the Grand Lodge of the Antients in England, established in 1751. He authored their book of constitutions, entitled *Ahiman Rezon*, first printed in 1756.

Shawn Eyer is a Past Master and the current Worshipful Master of Academia Lodge № 847, F∴ & A∴M∴ of California, and edits *Ahiman* and other Plumbstone publications. He also serves as the editor of the quarterly magazine of the Philalethes Society, the oldest independent Masonic research organization in North America.

Jeremy Gross is the Junior Deacon of King Solomon's Lodge, A∴F∴ & A∴M∴, in Somerville, Massachusetts.

Mounir Hanafi is the Chaplain of Cape Coral Lodge № 367, F∴ & A∴M∴ of Florida.

Dick Hixson is a professional photographer in the San Francisco bay area, currently serving as the Worshipful Master of Martinez Lodge № 41, F∴ & A∴M∴ of California.

Brian Hodges is a Master Mason in Academia Lodge № 847, F∴ & A∴M∴ of California, and a reader for the Sublime Masters Guild of the Oakland Scottish Rite Temple, AASR–SJ.

Adam G. Kendall manages the Henry Wilson Coil Library and Museum of Freemasonry in San Francisco. He has been a presenter at the International Conference on the History of Freemasonry in Scotland and other scholarly gatherings in the United States. He is a Past Master of Phoenix Lodge № 144, F∴ & A∴M∴ of California.

Joseph Fort Newton (1880–1950) was the author of many valuable books of Masonic interpretation, and the first Editor of *The Builder*, the magazine of the National Masonic Research Society.

Gregory Maier is a writer living in the San Francisco Bay Area.

Erik O'Neal was raised in Edmond Lodge № 37, A∴F∴ & A∴M∴ of Oklahoma, and is a charter member of Veritas Lodge № 556 in Oklahoma City.

Gary Allan Peare is the Worshipful Master of Orinda Lodge № 122, F∴ & A∴M∴ of California.

David E. Stafford is a Past Master and the current Secretary of Bethpage Lodge № 521, F∴ & A∴M∴ of Tennessee. He is a charter member of Conlegium Ritus Austeri № 779, a traditional observance lodge in Nashville.

Thomas Starr King (1824–1864) was one of America's most legendary clergyman. He served as the Chaplain of San Francisco's Oriental Lodge № 144, F∴ & A∴M∴, and was the 1863 Grand Orator of the Grand Lodge of California.

W. L. Wilmshurst (1867–1939) was the author of many books and articles on the esoteric or philosophical aspects of Freemasonry. He was Worshipful Master of the Lodge of Harmony № 275 in Huddersfield, England, in 1909. In 1927 he founded The Lodge of Living Stones № 4957, a lodge devoted to contemplative Freemasonry.

Thomas D. Worrel is a Past Master of Mill Valley Lodge № 356, F∴ & A∴M∴ of California, and an associate member of the Lodge of Living Stones № 4957 in Leeds, England. He is also a Past Celebrant of the Golden State College of the Societas Rosicruciana in Civitatibus Fœderatis. W∴ Bro∴ Worrel is currently pursuing a Ph.D. in Western Esotericism at the University of Exeter.

Image Credits

7	Photo: Alex Staroseltsev.
19	Photo: Marie-Lan Nguyen.
20, 25	Photo: Michael Bretherton.
30	Photo: Wikimedia Commons.
37	Photo: Wikimedia Commons.
40	Detail, Halliwell Ms., c. 1390 CE.
41	Detail, Martianus Capella, *De Nuptiis Philologiae et Mercurii de Grammatica* (Vicenza: Henricus de Sancto Ursio, 16 Dec. 1499). Photo: Keio University.
43	Detail, colorized engraving of a Fellow Craft tracing board; after a design by John Harris (c. 1825).
46	Photo: Wikimedia Commons.
54	Photo: The Warburg Institute.
72	Photo: Domenico Pellegriti.
82	Jan Saenredam, *Antrum Platonicum*, 1604.
85	William Fringham, *Hieroglyphica*, 1755.
93	Photo: Henry Wilson Coil Library & Museum of Freemasonry, Grand Lodge of California.
95	Photo: Wikimedia Commons.
99	Photo: Adam Kendall.
103	Photo: Dick Hixson.
104	*Laws and Statutes of the Lodge of Aberdeen*, Scotland, 1670.
107	Title page, *The Free-Masons' Calendar*, 1775.
108	Photo: Thomas J. Monteforte.
109	Photo: Dick Hixson.
113	Frontispiece, *Jachin and Boaz*, 1776.
114	Photo: Andrew Horn.
118	Photo: Richard J. Powell. Property of the Grand Lodge F&AM, State of New York.
119	Photo: Thomas J. Monteforte.
126, 128, 129	Photo: Julian Rees.
130	Photo: Ferenc Sebök

Index

Abelson, Paul 59n

Aberdeen, Lodge of 104–105, 116n

Abraham (Biblical patriarch) 21

Adam (Biblical patriarch) 6, 45, 46, 47

Ahiman (Biblical character) 1–3, 8–9; meaning of name, 1; Laurence Dermott's vision of, 5–9

Ahiman: A Review of Masonic Culture & Tradition 1–4; purpose of, 1, 3–4

Ahiman Rezon (Constitutions of the Antients), 1756 edition 1, 2–3, 105, 107, 116n

Akiva, Rabbi 102

Akkub (Biblical character) 1, 2, 8

Alaric 41

alchemy 38–39, 49, 134

Alcoran *see* Kuran

allegorical figure, defined, 106–107; such figures in Masonry include Faith, Hope, Charity, Temperance, Fortitude, Prudence, Justice, Father Time, the Weeping Virgin, and Silence, 107

altar 108

America, first Masonic settlers in, 104, 116n

Anderson, James (Scottish glazier, father of Rev. James Anderson) 105

Anderson, Rev. James, (1679–1739) 2, 6, 47, 105, 116n; *Constitutions* (1723), 27n, 47, 105, 116n; *Constitutions* (1738), 27n

Angerona 107–108, 111, 118, 119

Antients 2, 3, 105, 107; 1751 seal of, 108

Aquinas, St. Thomas (1225–1274) 47

architectis 53

Aristeas 114–15

Aristotle 14, 15–16, 35

arithmetic 34, 36

Ars Quatuor Coronatorum 3, 117n

ars memoria see art of memory

art of memory 30f, 41, 53ff, 62ff

astrology 33–34, 36, 42, 50, 56, 57, 134

astronomy 23, 25, 33–34, 36ff, 43–44, 50, 52

audi, vide, tace (Latin motto) 114, 119n

Augustine of Hippo (354–430 CE) 52, 55, 61n

Avicenna / Ibn Sīnā (980–1037 CE) 55, 84

axis mundi 38, 40

Babylon 45

Ballou, Rev. Hosea (1771–1852) 20

Bancks, John (1709–1751) 107

Barber, Malcolm 49

Beatrice (*Divine Comedy*) 49

Beecher, Rev. Henry Ward (1813–1887) 90

Belgium 49

Benoit, Koren 92

Bernard of Clairvaux, St. (1090–1153) 46, 47f, 50; in Dante's *Divine Comedy*, 48–49, 50, 57

Blodgett, Peter J. 93n

Bogdan, Henrik, *Western Esotericism and Rituals of Initiation* (reviewed) 127–29

Book of Constitutions (symbolism) 112

Bowra, Maurice 16

Bromwell, H.P.H. (1823–1903) 33–34, 59n

Brown, Robert Hewitt 33–34, 59n

Bruno, Giordano (1548–1600) 55, 56f; memory wheels or palaces, 54–55

Budge, Sir E.A. Wallis (1857–1934) 59n

Bulwer-Lytton, Lord Edward George (1803–1873), 111, 118n

Bunyan, John (1628–1688) 10n

Burckhardt, Titus (1908–1984) 48, 51

cable-tow (Masonic symbol) 17

Cain (Biblical character) 8

Cairns, H. 86n

Calcott, Wellins (b. 1726) 107

California, Grand Lodge of 91; 1863 Grand Oration of, 94–101

Camillo, Giulio (1480–1544) 55–56

Carruthers, Mary 53–55

cardinal directions 108, 111

cardinal virtues 16, 80, 106; Biblical & Platonic references to, 80

Cassiodorus (480–575 CE) 35

celestial lodge 111; *see* celestial temple

celestial temple 51

chamber of reflection 117n

Chartres 36–38, 41, 46, 47–48, 51–54, 57

Christianity 35–36, 41, 49, 57, 70, 80, 98, 101, 132

Cicero 7, 18n

Cistercians 47–49, 51, 57

Clark, Sir John 6

Claudy, Carl H. (1879–1957) 28n
Compass (as a symbol) 24
Constantine I 41
Cooke MS. 46
cornerstone, Masonic laying of 111
Council of Troyes (1128) 48, 49
Cross, Jeremy Ladd (1783–1860) 47, 60n, 68, 112, 119n
d'Alviella, Count Eugène Goblet (1846–1925) 27n
d'Assigny, Fifield (1707–1744) 6, 118n
da Costa, Hippolyto (1774–1823) 81, 87n
Dante Alighieri (1265–1321) 42, 48–49, 50f, 52, 55, 57, 59n
David (Biblical king) 1
Dee, John (1527–1608) 133
degrees, Masonic
    1° Entered Apprentice 25–26, 83
    2° Fellow Craft 26, 31–35, 83–84
    3° Master Mason 85
    9° Elu of the Nine 82
    30° Knight Kadosh 32, 34, 50, 51
    Royal Ark Mariner 46
de Hoyos, Arturo 59n
de Molay, Jacques (c. 1240–1314) 49
Demosthenes (384–322 BCE) 6
Dermott, Laurence (1720–1791) 2–3, 107, 116n;
    Hebrew signature of, 10; "vision" of, 2–3; 5–10
Desaguliers, John Theophilus (1683–1744) 6
destitution, rite of 26
Dionysian mysteries 80
Dowland MS. 21, 45
Dryfhout, John H. 119n
Dyer, Colin F.W. (1910–1987) 86n, 108
Edinger, Edward F. 38–39, 59n
Egypt 39, 80
Eleusinian mysteries 80, 118n
Eliade, Mircea (1907–1986) 39–40, 59n
Elijah (Biblical prophet) 39
Emerson, Ralph Waldo (1803–1882) 24, 90
Emulation Rite, lectures of 16, 47
England 49
England, United Grand Lodge of 106; motto of, 114
esotericism 49, 57; Biblical 48
Euclid 21–22, 24, 36, 45; 47th problem of (symbolism), 28n
eureka 27n
Euripides 6
Fabre, Jean-Henri (1823–1915), 23–24, 28n

Faivre, Antione 49
Fideler, David R. 52, 61n
five, symbolism of 40
four, symbolism of 27n; see also cardinal virtues
France 49, 50
Freemasons' Hall (London) 106
Funde merum genio (Latin: "make a libation to the spirit") 105, 117n.
Galloway, James (d. 1806) 105–106
gematria 39, 52
geometry 31, 34, 36, 45, 52; physical, moral and spiritual 24
grammar 34, 36
Great Geometrician, God as 21, 24
Guénon, René (1886–1951) 50–51
Guthrie, Oklahoma, Scottish Rite Temple 108, 119
Guthrie, W.K.C. (1906–1981) 86n
Habakkuk (Biblical prophet) 114
Hall, Manly Palmer (1901–1990) 86n
Halliwell MS. 40–41, 45, 46
Ham (Biblical character), as second son of Noah, 8
Handfield-Jones, R.M. 46
Harelian MS. 21
Harpocates 107, 111; sign of, 111
Harvey, J.M. 117n
Haywood, Harry L. (1886–1956) 27n, 33, 58n, 84, 86n
Hebrew (language) 1, 10, 32, 50, 128
Hebron, Valley of 46
Heracles 39
Heredom: The Transactions of the Scottish Rite Research Society 3, 116n
Hermes Trismegistos 45, 46, 57, 58
Hermetic Order of the Golden Dawn 133, 134
hermeticism 56–58, 64, 131, 132–34
high priest 3, 8–9; bound by cable-tow on yom ha-kipurim, 17
Hill, William H. 101
Hiram Abiff 39
Hixson, Dick 110–11
Horace 6, 108
Horus 39
Horn, Andrew 115
hubris, defined by Aristotle 14
Hugh of Payens (1070–1136) 48–49
Hutchens, Rex R. 82, 86n
Hutchinson, William (1705–1777) 17, 107–108

installation ceremony (American) 112

Islam 10n, 40, 50, 84

Italy 47

Jachin and Boaz (1762) 112, 117n; 1776 edition,
 frontispiece of, 113

Jacks, Rev. Lawrence Pearsall (1860–1955) 28n

James, William (1842–1910) 28n

Jefferson, Thomas (1743–1826) 90

Jeremiah (Biblical prophet), called "Jerry" by
 Dermott, 7

Jerusalem 8, 40, 48, 114–15; *see* Temple at
 Jerusalem

Jesus 24, 39, 45, 48

Jones, Bernard E. 117n

Josephus 2, 6; called "Flavius" by Dermott, 7;
 Antiquities of the Jews, 1

kabbalah 3, 8, 10n, 34, 39, 56, 57, 59n, 130

Katzenellenbogen, Adolf (1901–1964) 36–37, 59n

key (symbolism) 108

King, Rev. Thomas Starr 89–93; Masonic oration
 of, 94–101; Masonic funeral of, 91

Kittredge, Alfred B. 93n

Klibansky, Raymond (1905–2205) 36, 37–38, 59n

Knights Templar *see* Order of the Temple

Kuran (Alcoran) 6, 10n

ladder (symbolism) 30; in Egyptian myth, 39;
 Jacob's dream of, 40; of Kadosh, 32, 50, 51

Lamech (Biblical character) 45

Lavine, T. Z. 81, 87n

Levites, 1

liberal arts and sciences 31ff; as levels of
 consciousness, 34; correspondences
 with lodge officers, 34; correspondences
 with planets, 50; defined, 35; Freemasons
 required to study, 31; in the Middle Ages,
 36; origination of, 35–36; personified
 representation of, 46–47; power to humanize,
 33; as preliminary to theology, 41; purpose
 was philosophical, 41; *see also* grammar,
 rhetoric, logic, arithmetic, geometry, music,
 astronomy)

lignam vitæ 117n

logic 34, 36

Logos 52

Lovejoy, Rev. Elijah Parish (1802–1837) 90

Luscombe, David E. 38, 59n

Lyon, David 6

Lyon, David Murray 115n

Mackey, Albert G. (1807–1881) 27n, 80, 83, 86n

MacNulty, W. Kirk 34, 59n

Marcus Aurelius 6

Martí, José (1853–1895) 19

Martianus Capella 41–42, 46, 59n

Meeson, William 15–16, 18n

Mercury 40, 41–42, 50

Metcalf, Abraham T. 115

Meyer, Ellsworth 93

Middle Chamber lecture 31–32, 43–44

Militia of Christ 49

Miller, A.L. 116n

Milton, John (1608–1674) 6

Mithraic mysteries 40

Moderns 2, 3, 105, 107–108

Moore, Charles Whitlock (1801–1873) 47

Moses (Biblical prophet) 3, 24

Mount Moriah, 26

Muhammad, 40

Muir, John (1838–1914), 91

music, 34, 36

Nails, Debra, 86n

Nebuchadnezar (Biblical king) 3

necromancy 45

Needleman, Jacob 60n

Newton, Rev. Joseph Fort, essay on "The
 Geometry of Character," 21–28

New York, Grand Lodge of 108, 118

neoplatonism 57, 64, 70n, 132–33

Noah (Biblical patriarch) 5, 9, 46, 55, 70

Old Charges 21,

Oliver, Rev. George (1782–1867) 111

Order of the Garter 49

Order of the Golden Fleece 49

Order of the Star 49

Order of the Temple 47, 49f, 57

Orphism 40

Osiris 39

Parker, Rev. Henry 90

Patigian, Haig (1876–1950) 89; statue of Starr
 King, 99

Peare, Gary Allan 91–92, 110–11

Pennell, John 6

Pennsylvania, Grand Lodge of 108, 118n

Phædrus 14

Philalethes Society 58

Pike, Albert (1809–1891) 34,, 59n, 79–80, 82–83,
 85, 86n

pillars, antedivulian 45–46, 57, 59n, 60n

pillars, seven of wisdom 31, 56

pillars, Solomonic (Jachin and Boaz) 69,

Plato 15, 16, 21–23, 35, 41; academy of, 21, 79–80; allegory of the cave, 73–78, engraving of, 82, Masonic interpretation of, 79–86; taught quadrivium, 41

Plato 15, 16, 18n, 21, 23, 35, 41, 59n, 64, 79–86, 87n; allegory of the cave, 72–78, 79–87

platonism 36, 38, 51–53, 55–57; see also neoplatonism

Portugal 49

Pound, Roscoe (1870–1964), 27n, 58n

Preston, William (1742–1818), 28n, 31, 60n, 62, 81, 107, 112, 128; lectures of, 16, 18n, 31, 43–44, 47, 58n, 62, 68, 85–86, 87n, 107, 112, 128

Pritchard, Samuel 133

Proclus 21

Protagoras 15, 18n

psychology 14, 34, 38–39, 127

Pythagoras 21, 23, 28n, 36, 45, 57, 102

Pythagoreanism 16, 36, 52, 56–57

quadrivium 36–37, 41; emphasized by the Chartres school, 37; preparation for highest form of knowledge, 41

Quakers see Society of Friends

Radford and Tunnah manuscript rituals, cited, 108–110

Rees, Julian 70, 127–31

Regius poem see Halliwell MS.

Remes, Paulina 70n

Republic 41

rhetoric 34, 36

Rodgers, John 90

Romberch, Johannes (1480–1532) 55

Rosicrucianism 111; see Societas Rosicruciana

Rush, William (1756–1833) 108, 109

Saint-Gaudens, Augustus (1848–1907) 118–19n

Saturn 40

Schaw Statutes, Second (1599) 57–58

Schaw, William (1550–1602) 58

Schuchard, Marsha Keith 57

Scotland 63, 104–105, 115–16n

Scott, John 6

Scottish Rite 82, 108; see degrees, Masonic

sefirot 56

Set 39

Seth (Biblical patriarch) 45, 59n

seven, as a sacred or mystical number 27n, 40, 51, 55–56

Shallum (Biblical character) 1, 8

shamanism 39–40

Shaw, Gregory 55

Simonds, William Day (1855–1920) 89, 90, 91, 92n, 93n

Simonides 13–15

Slosson, Edwin E. 24

Smart, Christopher (1722–1771) 14

Smith, William 6

Societas Rosicruciana 111; in Civitatibus Fœderatis, 118n

Society of Friends (Quakers), first Masonic settlers in America, 116n

Socrates 6, 73–78, 80

Solomon (Biblical king) 2, 3, 7, 43, 45, 47, 48, 59n, 97, 128

Solomon's Temple see Temple at Jerusalem

Spratt, Edward 6

Square (symbolism) 12, 15–17, 108, 111

staircase lecture see Middle Chamber lecture

Steinmetz, George H. 34, 59n

Stevenson, David 57–58, 116n

Street, Oliver Day (1866–1944) 27n

sublimatio 38–39

Sumner, Charles (1811–1874) 90

sword see Tiler, sword of

Talmon (Biblical character) 1, 8

Talmud 1

Temple at Jerusalem 1–2, 7–8, 26, 45, 47, 51, 97, 114–15; antediluvian pillars and, 45; Aristeas' account of, 114–15; as prototype, 51–52; Holy of Holies of, 17; use of in the art of memory, 41, 56

Temple, Celestial, 26–27

Theodosius 41

theoreticus 53

theurgy 55

Thierry of Chartres (d. 1150) 37

Thoreau, Henry David (1817–1862) 90

Thoth 45

three, symbolism of, 27n, 40

Three Distinct Knocks (1760) 117n, 118n

Tiler, duties of, 112; sword of, 112

Toz Graecus 45

tracing boards 68, 70, 127–131, 133

Tringham, William 85, 107–108, 118n

trivium 36
Tree of Life 17, 34
Trestle-Board (symbolism) 27
troubadors 50
Tubal-Cain (Biblical character) 45
Tyler *see* Tiler
Tyre 8
vide, aude, tace (Latin motto) 112–14, 115
Virgil (70–19 BCE) 6, 49; in Dante's *Divine Comedy*, 49
Volume of the Sacred Law 27

Waite, Arthur Edward (1857–1942) 27n
Ward, John Sebastian Marlow (1885–1949) 27n
Webb, Thomas Smith (1771–1819) 47
Wendte, Rev. Charles William (1844–1931) 89
Wilmshurst, W. L. (1867–1939) 16, 27n, 34–35, 59n, 80, 86n, 87, 106, 117n
winding stairs, symbolism of 33–35
Yates, Dame Frances Amelia (1899–1981) 55–56, 57
Zohar (*Sefer ha-Zohar*) 17, 18n, 133
Zoroaster 45

Index of Traditional Sources

BIBLE, APOCRYPHA & PSEUDEPIGRAPHA

1 Chronicles	9:17–19, 22–31	1–2
Ecclesiastes	9:8	9
Habakkuk	2:20	114
Joshua	15:14	1
Numbers	13:22	1
Proverbs	8:27	24
	9:1	31
	26:11	83
Psalms	121:1	87
	133:1	96
Wisdom of Ben Sirach	6: 33–34	9, 10
	32:1–3	9
Wisdom of Solomon	8:5–7	80
1 Corinthians	12:26	96
2 Corinthians	5:1	26, 51
Romans	14:7	96
Life of Adam & Eve	50.1–2	45, 59n
	50.3–8	45, 59n
Chronicles of Jerahmeel	32.4	45

TALMUD

Babylonian Talmud		
Sotah	34b	1
Yoma	10a	1
Pirke Avot	3:13	102

KABBALAH

Zohar	3.102a	17

CLASSICAL MATERIALS

Aristeas	92, 94–95, 99	114–15
Aristotle		
Nichomachean Ethics	1100b21–22	18n
Rhetoric	1378b	14
Cicero		
De Oratore	2.86	18n
Horace		
Odes	3.2.25–28	108
Josephus		
Antiquities of the Jews	3.14	1
Simonides	4.1–21	13–14
Stobæus	frag. 24	102
Phædrus	20.43–46	14
Philo of Alexandria		
On the Creation of the World 97		12
Plato		
Phædo	69a–d	80
Protagoras	339a–344b	15
Republic	514b–518d	73–78
	515e	84
	516a	84
	516a–b	85
	522a–528e	41
Timæus	22b	80

The Square and Compass Mortality Ring. *A dedication to the Third Degree. Featuring a beehive with three bees, a sword pointing to a naked heart, a divine triangle with an All Seeing Eye, and the three steps, the ring is surmounted by a pentagonal crest featuring the Square and Compass, and a gemstone or centerpiece of your choice. Also available with the casket crest holding a skull and bones.*

The Revere Jewel.
The original of this 2" decorative Masonic jewel was rumored to be created by Bro. Paul Revere for Bro. George Washington. The Jewel features several working tools in an arranged composition.

The Renaissance Jewel
Presented as a rather large 4" display jewel, with faux leather pouch and blue silk ribbon.

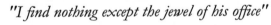

The Archway Ring *is directly inspired by the Royal Arch Degree. The ring features the Square and Compass set upon a stone arch-way, with a Keystone in the top. Underneath the archway, on the sides, is placed a representation of the Ark of the Covenant above flowing acacia leaves.*

"I find nothing except the jewel of his office"

The Master's Jewel

Proudly Serving the Craft since 2001.

Handcrafted Masonic Rings and Fine Jewels

Please visit our website, call us at 661-242-2374 or email us at studio@mastersjewel.com to request our new 16 page full color Masonic Jewelry catalog.

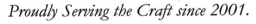

w w w . m a s t e r s j e w e l . c o m

Plumbstone

Quality Books for the Exploration of Freemasonry

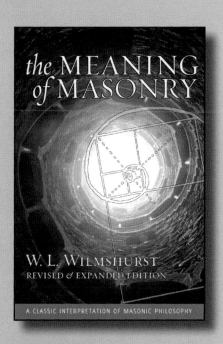

W.L. Wilmshurst's powerful vision of the rites and rituals of Freemasonry as a spiritual philosophy begins with this book. Here, Masonry is presented as "a sacramental system," represented not only by the ceremonies as experienced in the initiations, but also by an internal and mystical side, hidden behind the visible symbolism. This new, revised edition features a more readable modern typeface, and is enriched with extensive notes to make many of its points more accessible for both British and American students of Freemasonry.

Paperback, 192 pages
$19.97 USA & Canada
ISBN-13: 978-1-60302-000-8

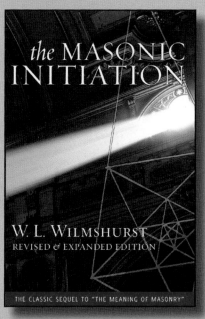

Here, we find Wilmshurst's most advanced expression as he explores the profound depths of Masonic ritual as a contemplative art, and offers his vision of the future of the Order. Both Freemasons and those who study the Craft from a distance will enjoy these insightful essays. Robert G. Davis writes in the Foreword that this edition provides "a new look at a timeless classic which has induced many generations of Masons to feel that, when they are in the sacred space of lodge, they are in the presence of a mystery that goes to the root of their own being."

Paperback, 208 pages
$19.97 USA & Canada
ISBN-13: 978-1-60302-002-2

Now available from: amazon.com   BARNES&NOBLE.com
www.bn.com